TRANSLATIONS OF EARLY DOCUMENTS
SERIES I
PALESTINIAN JEWISH TEXTS
(PRE-RABBINIC)

THE APOCALYPSE OF ABRAHAM

THE APOCALYPSE OF ABRAHAM

EDITED, WITH A TRANSLATION FROM THE SLAVONIC
TEXT AND NOTES

BY

G. H. BOX, M.A.

LECTURER IN RABBINIC HEBREW, KING'S COLLEGE, LONDON;
HON. CANON OF ST. ALBANS

WITH THE ASSISTANCE OF

J. I. LANDSMAN

WIPF & STOCK · Eugene, Oregon

Wipf and Stock Publishers
199 W 8th Ave, Suite 3
Eugene, OR 97401

Apocalypse of Abraham
Together with The Ascension of Isaiah
By Box, G. H. and Landsman, J. I
Softcover ISBN-13: 978-1-6667-6658-5
Hardcover ISBN-13: 978-1-6667-6659-2
Publication date 12/2/2022
Previously published by SPCK, 1919

This edition is a scanned facsimile of
the original edition published in 1919.

EDITORS' PREFACE

The object of this series of translations is primarily to furnish students with short, cheap, and handy text-books, which, it is hoped, will facilitate the study of the particular texts in class under competent teachers. But it is also hoped that the volumes will be acceptable to the general reader who may be interested in the subjects with which they deal. It has been thought advisable, as a general rule, to restrict the notes and comments to a small compass; more especially as, in most cases, excellent works of a more elaborate character are available. Indeed, it is much to be desired that these translations may have the effect of inducing readers to study the larger works.

Our principal aim, in a word, is to make some difficult texts, important for the study of Christian origins, more generally accessible in faithful and scholarly translations.

In most cases these texts are not available in a cheap and handy form. In one or two cases texts have been included of books which are available in the official Apocrypha; but in every such case reasons exist for putting forth these texts in a new translation, with an Introduction, in this series.

* * * * *

An edition of *The Apocalypse of Abraham* is included in the present volume. The explanatory notes, in this case, given in the commentary on the text, are rather longer and fuller than usual. This was rendered necessary by the fact that the Book is made accessible here to English readers for the first time; and the difficulties and obscurities in the text are not inconsiderable.

W. O. E. OESTERLEY.
G. H. BOX.

INTRODUCTION

Short Account of the Book

The Apocalypse of Abraham, which has been preserved in old Slavonic literature, falls into two distinct parts (cf. the somewhat similar case of *The Ascension of Isaiah*). The first part, contained in chaps. i.–viii., consists of a Midrashic narrative based upon the legend of Abraham's conversion from idolatry, which has several peculiar features.[1] The second part (chaps. ix.–xxxii.) is purely apocalyptic in character, and contains a revelation made to Abraham about the future of his race, after his (temporary) ascent into the heavenly regions, under the guidance of the archangel Jaoel, who here seems to play the part of Metatron-Michael. It is based upon the account of Abraham's trance-vision described in Genesis xv.—a favourite theme for apocalyptic speculation. In the Book, as it lies before us, the two parts are organically connected. Thus in chap. x. the archangel says: *I am the one who was commissioned to set on fire thy father's house together with him, because he displayed reverence for dead (idols)*—an allusion to the narrative of chap. viii.; and the general plan of the whole work seems to be based upon the idea that Abraham's dissatisfaction with the idol-worship by which he was surrounded, which found vent in his strong protest to his father Terah (chaps. i.–viii.), appealed so much to the divine favour, that the archangel Jaoel was specially sent

---

[1] See Appendix I, esp. p. 93.

by God to instruct him and initiate him into the knowledge of heavenly mysteries. Whether the apocalyptic portion ever existed in a shorter and independent form will be discussed below.

The Book opens with a description of Abraham's activities as a maker and seller of idols, his father Terah being a manufacturer of idols. His doubts as to the justifiable character of the idol-worship are roused especially by an accident that befell the stone image called Merumath, and by a similar accident that happened to " five other gods," by which they were broken in pieces (chaps. i.–ii.). Reflecting on this, he is led to protest to his father against the unreality of asking a blessing from such helpless images, thereby rousing Terah's anger (chaps. iii.–iv.). He is led to test further the powers of the idols by placing a wooden god *Barisat* before the fire, and telling the idol to see that the fire must not be allowed to die down during his absence. On returning he finds *Barisat* fallen backwards and " horribly burnt " (chap. v.). He again protests to his father against the futility of such worship, sarcastically contrasting the relative merits of gold, silver and wooden idols (chap. vi.). He then proceeds to show that the elements of fire, water, earth, and the heavenly bodies (sun, moon, and stars) are more worthy of honour than the idols, and yet, as each is subjected to some superior force, they can none of them claim to be God (chap. vii.). While he was yet speaking to his father a voice came from heaven bidding him leave his father's house. He had scarcely left the house when fire descended and consumed all within it.

The apocalyptic part opens with a divine command to Abraham to prepare a sacrifice with a view to receiving a divine revelation concerning the future (chap. ix.). Abraham, terrified at the experience, is confronted by the angel Jaoel, who encourages him, and explains his commission to be with Abraham, and act as his celestial guide. Under the direction of the angel he proceeds to Horeb, the Mount of God, a journey of forty days (chaps. x.–xii.), and there, with the help of Jaoel, accomplishes the sacrifice. At this point Azazel, the fallen archangel and seducer of mankind, intervenes and attempts to dissuade Abraham from his purpose. In the form of an unclean bird he flies down "upon the carcasses" (cf. Gen. xv. 11), and tries to induce Abraham to leave the holy place, but in vain. Jaoel denounces the evil spirit, bidding him depart, and telling him that the heavenly garment which was formerly his has been set aside for Abraham (chaps. xiii.–xiv.).

After this Abraham and the angel ascend on the wings of the unslaughtered birds (of the sacrifice) to heaven, which is described at length. It is filled with "a strong light" of power inexpressible, and there they see the angels who are born and disappear daily, after singing their hymn of praise (chaps. xv.–xvi.). At this point Abraham, hearing the divine voice, falls prostrate, and, taught by the angel, utters the celestial song of praise, and prays for enlightenment (chap. xvii.). He sees the divine throne with the Cherubim and the holy Creatures (*ḥayyoth*), of whom a description is given, and particularly of their rivalry which is mitigated by the activity of Jaoel (chap. xviii.). God now speaks and discloses to Abraham the powers of heaven in the various firmaments below (chap. xix.). God promises him a seed numerous as the stars (chap. xx.). In answer to a question by Abraham about Azazel, God shows him a vision of the world, its fruits and creatures, the sea and its monsters (including Leviathan), the Garden of Eden, its fruits, streams, and blessedness. He sees also a multitude of human beings "half of them on the right side of the picture, and half of them on the left" (chap. xxi.). The fall of man is explained to him, being traced to the sin of Adam and Eve in the Garden, a vision of which appears in the picture and also of its results upon the destinies of mankind, who are divided into the people on the right side of the picture, representing the Jewish world, and the people on the left representing the heathen world. In particular the sin of idolatry resulting in impurity and murder is sketched and made manifest (chaps. xxii.–xxv.). The question, why sin is permitted, is answered by God (chap. xxvi.), and this is followed by a vision of judgement in which the destruction of the Temple is pourtrayed. In answer to Abraham's anguished question it is explained to him that this is due to the sin of idolatry on the part of his seed. At the same time a hint is given him of coming salvation (chap. xxvii.). In answer to the question, how long shall the judgement last? a description is given of the troubles preceding the Messianic Age, and the dawn of the latter (chaps. xxviii.–xxix.; the latter chapter contains a long Christian interpolation). At this point Abraham finds himself "upon the earth," but receives a further disclosure regarding the punishment of the heathen and the ingathering of Israel (chaps. xxx.–xxxi.). A short paragraph repeating the promise of the chosen people's deliverance from oppression closes the Book (chap. xxxii.).

The character of the Book, as a whole, is thoroughly Jewish. Its original language was probably Hebrew or Aramaic, from which a Greek version (underlying the Slavonic) was made; and the date of the original composition may be placed at the end of the first or the beginning of the second century A.D.

THE SLAVONIC TEXT AND MSS [1]

The Slavonic version, or rather translation, of *The Apocalypse of Abraham* (*Ap. Abr.*) has been preserved in a number of MSS. The oldest and most valuable of these is the famous Codex Sylvester,[2]

[1] The substance of this section of the Introduction has been contributed by Mr. J. I. Landsman.

[2] Sylvester, after whom the MS. is named, was a prominent priest in the early years of the reign of Ivan the Terrible,

INTRODUCTION xi

which now belongs to the Library of the Printing-department of the Holy Synod in Moscow. The MS., which dates from the first half of the fourteenth century, is written on parchment, with two columns on each page, and contains 216 leaves in all, our Apocalypse occupying leaves 164–182.[1] It contains a collection of lives of different saints, and *The Apocalypse of Abraham* stands in it as a work complete in itself, without any connexion with the works which precede and follow it.

The text of our Apocalypse according to Codex Sylvester (cited as S) has been edited by Professor N. Tikhonravov in his *Memorials of Russian Apocryphal Literature* (*Pamyatniki otrechennoi russkoi literatury*), Moscow, 1863, Vol. I. pp. 32–53; and also Professor J. Sreznevsky in his *Ancient Monuments of Russian Writing and Language* (*Drevnie Pam'yatniki russkovo pis'ma i yazyka*), Petrograd, 1863, I. pp. 247[b]–256[a], with readings from the Uvaroff MS., which apparently is a mere copy of S. Tikhonravov has supplied his edition with corrections of the numerous clerical mistakes which abound in S, thereby earning the gratitude of students, while Sreznevsky has satisfied himself with producing a mere copy of the text, with all its mistakes. Apart from these editions there has also been published by the Imperial Society of Bibliophiles a facsimile edition of the text of our Apocalypse, according to S (Petrograd, 1890), thus affording students the means of consulting the MS. itself. Apart from S the

---

upon whom he for some years exercised a salutary influence. He was an author and lover of books, and the Codex was one of a collection of MSS. which remained after his death in the Kirillo monastery, whither he was banished: see Sreznevsky, *Narratives about the Saints Boris and Gleb* (*Skazania o sv'yatykh Borisĕ i Glĕbĕ*), Petrograd, 1860, Pt. I., and *The Orthodox Encyclopædia* (*Pravoslavnaya Bogoslovskaya E.*) iv. 1195 (*s.v. Domostroi*).

[1] A full description of S is given by Sreznevsky, *op. cit.*, pp. i–viii.

text of *Ap. Abr.* is also contained in many *Palæas*.[1] The Palæa, as its name indicates (ἡ παλαιά sc. διαθήκη), deals with the Old Testament, especially with the historical part of it, beginning with creation and ending with David or Solomon, the biblical narratives being enlarged and embellished with apocryphal and pseudepigraphical matter. The origin of the Slavonic Palæa must be sought in some Greek prototype,[2] which by way of Bulgaria and Serbia had, at an early date, found an entrance into Russia, where for centuries it enjoyed great popularity—at least so long as a translation of the whole Bible had not been made accessible to both clergy and people, that is up till the sixteenth century.

There are two kinds of Palæas, the historical and the expository, the former being also known as the "eyes" of the Palæa, because it contains the text upon which the expository Palæa comments. The expositions are of a polemical character, the polemic being invariably directed against the Jews (*Zhidovin*), to whom it is demonstrated that all the prophecies and the manifold types had found their true fulfilment in Christ. The Palæa draws richly upon the Jewish Midrashic Literature, and then uses the material as an argument against the Jews from whom it was borrowed.

Originally our Apocalypse had no place in the Palæa, as may be seen from the oldest Palæa MS., which dates from the fourteenth century, and is preserved in the Alexander-Nevsky Monastery (Petrograd). Later, it was inserted, but still retained its original character of an independent work (as is the case in the Uvaroff Palæa); but later still

[1] On the subject of the Palæa see the works of N. S. Tikhonravov (*Sochinenia*), Moscow, 1898, Vol. I. pp. 156–170, and the valuable notes at the end of the volume; cf. also the article *Palæa* in the Russian Encyclopædia published by Brockhaus—Efron.

[2] A MS. of a Greek Palæa is known to exist in the Vienna Library, and has been edited by A. V. Vasil'eff in *Anecdota græco-byzantina*, I. pp. 188–192 (Moscow, 1892).

INTRODUCTION

(from the sixteenth century and onwards) the text of *Ap. Abr.* loses its original character of an independent work, the material being worked into the life of Abraham. The title of the Book is dropped, and the first person in which Abraham speaks in S is altered into the third, that is, it is changed into a narrative about Abraham, though the scribe often forgets himself and retains the first person of the original.

The apocryphal and pseudepigraphical writings must have been introduced into Russia at a very early date. Large parties of devout Russians, conducted by some learned monk, made frequent pilgrimages to Constantinople and the Holy Land. It was on such pilgrimages that the people were, for the first time, made acquainted with these writings, and the learned monk would, on the spot, translate the book, which had enriched his knowledge concerning the Patriarchs or the Apostles, into Slavonic, and then bring it back, as a most precious treasure to his own country, to the great delight of his fellow-monks in the monastery. It may, therefore, be taken for granted that the Greek original of our Apocalypse had never been brought to Russia, and that there never existed more than one translation of it into Slavonic, for S and the Palæa do not represent different translations, but only different types or recensions of one and the same version. The differences between the Palæa and S are very slight, the former only modernising here and there the style and the orthography. The Palæa is, therefore, of great value for the reconstruction of the original text, especially as it has preserved, in many cases, a more correct copy than is the case with S. The Palæa version is, however, disfigured by the many interpolations made by subsequent scribes which are all absent from S, and which are easily discernible as being interpolations.[1]

[1] Matter which is not found in S is, in the translation printed below, enclosed in square brackets, and printed in smaller type.

xiv INTRODUCTION

The Palæa version of our Apocalypse has been edited by Tikhonravov[1] from a MS. which once belonged to the Joseph-Monastery in Volokolamsk, whence it has been transferred to the Library of the Moscow Academy of Divinity,[2] the MS. dating from the fifteenth century. Then I. Porfir'ev edited it in his *Apocryphal Narratives about Old Testament Persons and Events* (*Apokrificheskia skazania o vetkhozavetnykh litsakh i sobytiakh*), Petrograd, 1877, pp. 111–130,[3] from a MS. dating from the seventeenth century, originally the property of the Library of the Solovetzk-Monastery, whence it was transferred to the Library of the Kasan Academy of Divinity.[4] A and K are closely related to each other, and represent a type of text common to them both. Thus the same mistakes are found in both, and also the same additional matter, not extant in S.[5]

Another Palæa-text, containing part of the text of our Apocalypse, viz. the legendary narrative in chaps. i.–viii. only, has been edited by A. Pypin in *Pseudepigrapha and Apocrypha of Russian Antiquity* (*Ložnyja i otrechennyja knigi russkoi stariny*) in the third volume of Kuselev-Bezborodko, *Memorials of Old Russian Literature* (*Pam'yatniki starinnoj russkoi literatury*), Petrograd, 1882, pp. 24–26. This is from the Palæa of the Rumjancov Museum, dating from the year 1494.[6]

In S the end of the Book is missing, but is, fortunately, extant both in A and K. K also has at the end a short paragraph not found in A, which forms an appropriate conclusion to the whole Book. The reader will find it given in the notes on

[1] *Op. cit.*, pp. 54–77.
[2] Cited below as A.
[3] Forming part of Vol. XVII, published by the Department of the Russian Language and Literature of the Imperial Academy of Sciences.
[4] Cited below as K.
[5] For some examples of identical errors in the text which appear in both A and K see Bonwetsch, p. 8.
[6] Cited as R below.

INTRODUCTION

the concluding passage. See further Appendixes II. and III.[1]

DATE OF COMPOSITION AND ORIGINAL LANGUAGE OF THE BOOK

The Slavonic text, it is obvious, was made from a Greek version which, no doubt, was current in Constantinople. It is probable, however, that the Greek text underlying the Slavonic was itself a translation of a Semitic original. A number of indications suggest this. The simple co-ordination of the sentences, the naïve repetitions, and the frequency of the phrase " Here am I " (= Hebrew *hinnēnî*), which characterise all parts of the Book, point in this direction. Then, too, the sarcastic names given to the idols in the first part (chaps. i.–viii.) —the stone idol *Merumath* (= *'eben Měrūmā*, " stone of deceit "), the wooden idol *Barisat* (= *bar 'ishtā* " son of the fire," Aramaic)—presuppose a knowledge of Hebrew or Aramaic, or both, on the part of the original readers which would hardly be likely in a purely Greek composition. The fact, too, that Abraham is supposed to be the speaker throughout may lend some weight to the argument for a Hebrew original. The cumulative effect of these considerations taken in conjunction with the intensely Jewish character of the Book as a whole makes a Semitic original highly probable. Perhaps the Book was composed in Hebrew, with a slight admixture of Aramaic, such as occurs in the early Palestinian Midrashim.

The date of the composition of the Book can be determined, within narrow limits, with some probability. Clearly the *terminus a quo* is the destruction of the Temple in Jerusalem in 70 A.D. which is bewailed by Abraham in the apocalyptic part of the Book. The fact, too, that it forms the central

[1] See further, Bonwetsch, pp. 1–11.

point of the picture, that the revelation leads up to it as a sort of climax, and that the apocalyptist is so deeply moved at the disclosure, suggests that the event is fairly recent. Ginzberg (*J.E.*, i. 92) thinks " the last decades of the first century " are probably the period to which the composition of the Book should be assigned, at any rate in its earliest form. In any case the *terminus ad quem* can hardly be later than the first decades of the second century. The fact that the Book won acceptance in Christian circles, and was adapted by slight interpolation to Christian purposes—though its intensely Jewish character is manifest on every page—strongly supports the early date. Such a Book would have appealed to Jewish-Christians in Palestine, when Jewish-Christianity was still in close touch with a non-Christian Jewish community in the Holy Land— and it may be assumed, in view of the Semitic character of its original language, that the Book was of Palestinian origin. It must, therefore, have been produced at a time when early apocalyptic literature was still being written in Hebrew or Aramaic, *i. e.* not later than the early decades of the second century.[1]

The question as to the existence of the Book at first in a shorter and much simpler form is discussed below.

Early Attestation of the Book

That the Book must have enjoyed some considerable vogue and popularity in certain Christian circles is proved by its survival, in more than one form, in old Slavonic literature. And this must be equally true of the Greek form of the Book from which the Slavonic was derived. There is, as we should expect, some early evidence of the Book's existence, though some of it is vague and uncertain. What seems to

[1] See *E.A.*, p. lviii ff.

INTRODUCTION xvii

be the clearest and most explicit piece of evidence of this kind is found in the Clementine *Recognitions*, I. 32, which carries us back to at least the early part of the fourth century, and which, not improbably, through the sources of the Clementine Literature, may go back to an earlier period, still, perhaps another century.[1] The section in the *Recognitions* deals with Abraham, and the part which specially concerns us runs as follows:

From the first this same man [Abraham], being an astrologer, was able, from the account and order of the stars, to recognise the Creator, while all others were in error, and understood that all things are regulated by His providence. Whence also an angel, standing by him in a vision, instructed him more fully concerning those things which he was beginning to perceive. He shewed him also what belonged to his race and posterity, and promised them that those districts should be restored rather than given to them.

Here the first sentence clearly refers to some form of the legend of Abraham's conversion from idolatry; but it agrees rather with Philo's account in *de Abrahamo*, § 15 (see Appendix I.) than with that embodied in the first part of our Book, which depicts Abraham in his early days as a maker and seller of idols rather than as an astrologer. But the second sentence forms a good description of the second or apocalyptic part of our Book, and may be taken as a reference to it. That in fact a book known as " the Apocalypse of Abraham " existed in his time is explicitly stated by Epiphanius (*Hær.* xxxix. 5) where, in speaking of the Gnostic sect called " the Sethians," he says they possessed a number of books " written in the name of great men," seven in the name of Seth, and among others one " in the name of Abraham which they also declare to be an apocalypse," and which is "full of all wickedness " (πάσης κακίας ἔμπλεων). Schürer thinks that this heretical book cannot be identified with our Apocalypse.

[1] Cf. Hort, *Clementine Recognitions*, pp. 80 ff.

xviii   INTRODUCTION

Dr. M. R. James, however,[1] is inclined to believe "that Epiphanius on his authority is here going too far, and is fathering on the Sethians a book, which they may well have used, but which they did not manufacture." It is quite possible, and not improbable that this Gnostic sect made use of our Book in an interpolated form. As we shall see, there are Gnostic features in it in the form in which it has reached us, and Ginzberg is inclined to regard these as interpolations from a Gnostic book bearing the same name. A heretical Book (or Apocalypse) of Abraham may also possibly be referred to in a passage in the *Apostolic Constitutions*, vi. 16 (compiled in its present form probably in the second half of the fourth century), which runs as follows:

And among the Ancients also some have written apocryphal books of Moses, and Enoch, and Adam, and Isaiah, and David, and Elijah, and of the three patriarchs, pernicious and repugnant to the truth (φθοροποιὰ καὶ τῆς ἀληθείας ἐχθρά).

It will be noticed that this is a list of Old Testament Pseudepigrapha, most of the items of which are easily recognisable. By "the three patriarchs" can only be meant Abraham, Isaac, and Jacob. Thus the passage attests the existence, at the time when the compiler wrote, of an apocryphal Book of Abraham, which may well be identical with our Apocalypse.[2] Lastly there is the evidence of the lists of books (containing the bare names) included in the *Synopsis of Pseudo-Athanasius*) compiled probably about 500 A.D.) and the Stichometry of Nicephorus (drawn up in Jerusalem perhaps about 850 A.D.). The latter is identical with the former, except that it attaches to the name of each book the number of *stichoi* or lines contained in it. The first six names

---

[1] *The Testament of Abraham* (Cambridge "Texts and Studies"), p. 14.

[2] It might, of course, refer to some other apocryphal Book of Abraham; Dr. M. R. James thinks the reference may be to *The Testament of Abraham*.

INTRODUCTION

on these lists are as follows: (1) *Enoch;* (2) *Patriarchs;* (3) *Prayer of Joseph;* (4) *Testament of Moses;* (5) *Assumption of Moses;* (6) *Abraham.* The second list adds to the sixth name "stichometry 300," thus giving us "a book [of Abraham] rather shorter than the Greek Esther, which has 350 στίχοι." Dr. M. R. James[1] is of opinion that the word ἀποκάλυψις is to be supplied before Ἀβραάμ here, and this view we may safely accept. We have thus another piece of evidence of the existence of a Book called "the Apocalypse of Abraham," which was of sufficient importance to be included in a list of books of Old Testament apocrypha containing such well-known names as the Book of Enoch, the Testaments of the Twelve Patriarchs, and the Assumption of Moses.

From a survey of this evidence it may be concluded that an apocryphal book (or books) under the name of Abraham was current in the early Christian centuries; and that our Apocalypse is one product or form of this literature. The so-called *Testament of Abraham* is, no doubt, another. The possibility remains to be considered that our Apocalypse may have assumed different forms (by enlargement or curtailment) and have been adapted at different times for different purposes.

GNOSTIC ELEMENTS IN THE TEXT

Among the Gnostic features in the text of our Book may be reckoned the significant emphasis laid upon "right" and "left" in the apocalyptic representation (cf. xxii. (end), xxiii.), the "right" side being the source of purity and light, the "left" that of impurity and darkness. This idea is ancient,[2] depending upon the dualism which insists upon the category of light and darkness, and can be traced back to ancient Zoroastrianism. But it was developed in the early Gnostic systems (see Irenæus, *adv. Hær.* I., xi. 2; II. xxiv. 6), and in the Jewish

[1] *Op. cit.*, p. 9. The synopsis embraces eleven items.
[2] Cf. Matt. xxv.

Kabbalah, where "right side" and "left side" (*siṭrā yêmînā wĕ-siṭrā 'aḥārā*) become technical terms. In the Emanistic system of the Zohar, the whole world is divided between "right" and "left," where pure and impure powers respectively operate—on the right side the Holy One and His powers, on the left the serpent Sammael and his powers (cf. Zohar, *Bereshith*, 47*b*, 53*f*, 169*b* and following, 174*b*). When, therefore, we find our Book dividing mankind into two hosts, one on the right side (= the Jews) and one on the left (= the heathen), the presence of Gnostic influence seems clear. At the same time, it may well be an original feature of the Book, as the idea had already been assimilated by the ancient Jewish mystical tradition (Kabbalah), and if our Apocalypse was of Essene origin there would be nothing surprising in the presence of such an element.

The opposition between light and darkness seems also to be present in an obscure passage in chap. xiv., which is absent from S. It runs as follows (Azazel is being addressed):

For thy heritage is (to be) over those existing with thee being born with the stars and clouds, with the men whose portion thou art, and (who) through thy being exist; and thine enmity is justification.

Perhaps by those "being born with the stars and clouds" is meant those who by birth and creation belong to the sphere of night and darkness, as opposed to the righteous who belong to the sphere of light. This again accords with the ancient dualistic conception referred to above, and may very well be an original feature. The absence of the clause from S may be due to excision. It can hardly be an interpolation from Slavonic sources.

On the other hand, there are two passages where the original text may have been modified under Christian Gnostic influence (apart from the obvious interpolation indicated by italic type in chap. xxix.). In chap. xx. God, addressing Abraham, says: " As the number of the stars and their power, (so will) I

INTRODUCTION

make thy seed a nation, and a people set apart for me in my heritage *with Azazel*." And again in chap. xxii. : " But those which are on the right side of the picture—they are the people set apart for me of the peoples *with Azazel*." Here God is represented as sharing His heritage (= the Jewish people) with the evil spirit Azazel. " This," says Ginzberg (*J.E.*, i. 92), " is no doubt the Gnostic doctrine of the God of the Jews as kakodaimon," *i. e.* that the God of the Old Testament is an inferior deity, whose work was fused with evil elements. Still, these Gnostic elements in our Book are not very pronounced; there are no clear and explicit allusions to any of the full-blown doctrines of the Ophites or kindred Gnostic sects. The phenomena suggest that the Book is an essentially Jewish one, which may have been used and read by Gnostic Christians, and adapted by slight revision to make it acceptable to such readers.

General Character of the Book and Integrity of its Text

The Book is essentially Jewish, and there are features in it which suggest Essene origin; such are its strong predestinarian doctrine, its dualistic conceptions, and its ascetic tendencies. It may well have passed from Essene to Ebionite circles—the interpolation in chap. xxix. certainly looks like the work of a Jewish-Christian—and thence, in some form, have found its way into Gnostic circles.

Is the Book as it lies before us—apart from the interpolation in chap. xxix.—substantially in its original shape? To this question an affirmative answer may, with some probability, be given. Ginzberg, it is true, suggests a different view. He says (*J.E.*, i. 92):

It is quite probable that certain parts of the heretical Apocalypse of Abraham, which was in circulation among the Gnostics (Epiphanius, xxxix. 5), were incorporated in the

INTRODUCTION

present text [of our Apocalypse]. Subtracting, then, the first part [*i. e.* chaps. i.–viii., containing the "Legend"], which does not belong to the Apocalypse, and the Gnostic and Christian interpolations, only about three hundred lines remain, and this number would exactly correspond with the number which, according to the stichometry of Nicephorus, the Apocalypse of Abraham contained.

There are considerable difficulties attaching to this theory. It is difficult to suppose that the Book in its original form was without the opening chapters (i.–viii.) narrating Abraham's conversion from idolatry. There are several allusions in the later chapters to this opening narrative, which come in quite naturally. The chapters form a good introduction to what follows, and, as such, were probably put into their present shape by the original author of the Book. The material of the legend was, of course, much older; but it is to be noticed that our author has handled this material in a very free way, and this fact also suggests that these chapters were no mere addition to the Book, borrowed from one of the current forms of the legend. It seems more probable that the shorter "Apocalypse of Abraham" implied by the Stichometry of Nicephorus was a shortened recension of the original book, probably adapted for orthodox Christian purposes. It is by no means impossible that a shorter recension may have existed side by side with the fuller original form at a later date. The latter may have survived and have been read in certain circles by preference, and thence have passed over into the old Slavonic Church literature. Whether the heretical "Apocalypse of Abraham" referred to by Epiphanius which, according to him was "full of all wickedness" was another and independent recension, it is impossible to say. On the whole it seems more likely that the older form of the Book—especially if it had grown up in Ebionite (Jewish-Christian) circles—was the form in which it was read by the Sethian Gnostics. The mere fact that it was read in such circles would make it suspicious in the eyes of a later orthodoxy, which may have endeavoured to suppress it by issuing a shorter recension of the text. But the older form was too popular to be eliminated in this way entirely—though it has almost disappeared from Christian literature, and in its Greek and Semitic forms has, in fact, disappeared, only surviving in its old Slavonic dress.

That such a Jewish-Christian Book would have been acceptable to Sethian Gnostic readers is not surprising. This Gnostic sect held the doctrine that the *Sophia* " found means to preserve through every age, in the midst of the Demiurge's world, a race bearing within them the spiritual seed which was related to her own nature " . . . they " regarded Cain as a representative of the Hylic; Abel, of the Psychical; and Seth, who was finally to reappear in the person of the Messiah, of the Pneumatic principle." [1]

The emphasis laid in our Book (chap. xxiv.) upon the lawlessness of Cain, " who acted lawlessly through the Adversary," and its evil consequence in the slaughter of Abel would appeal to such Gnostic readers no less than the division of mankind into " right " and " left," and the assignment of the latter to the dominion of the " lawless Adversary " Azazel. Abraham, too, the hero of the Book, was in the line of Seth, and it is from him that the Messiah springs (chap. xxix.). All this would be read by such Gnostic readers in the light of their own presuppositions.

We conclude, then, that the Book, substantially as it lies before us, is a Jewish and Essene production, like the related *Testament of Abraham*. It depicts the initiation of Abraham into the heavenly mysteries associated with the Divine " Chariot " (cf. Ezek. i.). Its angelology is in line with Essene speculation, and in chap. xvii. Abraham is taught by the archangel, in the form of the celestial hymn, the mystery of the Divine Name. We have reached the stage

[1] Neander, *Church History*, ii. 154.

when Enoch has fallen into the background, and Abraham, like Moses, has become the centre of mystic lore, that is "when the seal of circumcision had become the pledge of life."[1] It is noteworthy that the Kabbalistic book *Sefer Yeṣîrā* (? second century A.D.) was attributed to Abraham.

It may occur to some readers as an objection to this view that the prominence assigned to Abraham's sacrifice in the Book, and to the destruction of the Temple, regarded as the supreme calamity, is inconsistent with Essene authorship, since the Essenes rejected animal sacrifices. But, as Kohler has shewn,[2] the Essenes, who accepted the Mosaic Law, were not opposed to such sacrifices on principle. What they opposed was the priesthood in the Temple "out of mistrust as to their state of holiness and purity, rather than out of aversion to sacrifice." To Abraham, the Essene saint, acting under direct divine command, no such objection would apply.

It should be added that the Slavonic MSS. yield a text which is markedly shorter than the texts of the Palæan MSS. Some of the omitted passages are perhaps cases of deliberate excision, and others of accidental omission. But there remain a substantial number where the shorter text is probably original, and the presence of glosses or later amplifications is to be suspected. All such passages are indicated in the text of the translation given below.

THEOLOGY OF THE BOOK

The apocalyptic part of the Book is based upon the story of Abraham's sacrifice and trance, as described in Gen. xv. This experience is interpreted to mean that Abraham received a divine disclosure as to the destinies of his descendants, which is also the view of the Rabbinical Midrash (cf. *Bereshith rabba*, xliv. 15 f.). This scheme provides the framework in which our apocalypse is set.

[1] Cf. Kohler in *J.Q.R.*, vii. 594 (July 1895).
[2] In *J.E.*, v. 230 (s.v. *Essenes*).

INTRODUCTION xxv

Abraham, after completing the prescribed sacrifice, ascends to heaven, under the guidance of the angel, and from thence sees below him the drama of the world's future, and also the various powers and forces that operate in the celestial sphere. In exactly the same way the Midrash (*Bereshith rabba*, xliv. 14) interprets Abraham's experience as an ascension. According to a saying of R. Jehuda, citing the authority of R. Johanan, God *caused him* [Abraham] *to ascend above the vault of the firmament*, and said to him: "*Look now toward heaven*": "*looking* [*here*] *means nought else but from* [*the height*] *above to* [*what is*] *below*. This is a continuation of a comment on the sentence: *And He brought him forth outside* (Gen. xv. 5) interpreted to mean: "And He (God) brought him (Abraham) forth outside the world."

The angel who conducts Abraham on his celestial journey is the archangel Jaoel, who plays an all-important *rôle*. As is pointed out in the notes, he fulfils the functions elsewhere assigned to Michael and Metatron. Just as Metatron bears the tetragrammaton (cf. Ex. xxiii. 21, "My Name is in him)," so Jaoel here (chap. x.) is possessed of the power of the Ineffable Name. The name Jaoel itself is evidently a substitute for the tetragrammaton, which was too sacred to be written out in full. This angelic being is thus God's vicegerent, second only to God Himself. Yet he may not be worshipped, but rather himself sets Abraham the example of worshipping God. He is thus the supreme figure in Jewish angelology. Like Enoch, who was also transformed into Metatron, Jaoel acts as celestial guide. Jaoel is also the heavenly choir-master (chap. xii. "Singer of the Eternal"; cf. also chap. xvii.), a function assigned elsewhere to Michael; like Michael he is the guardian of the chosen race (chap. x., end), and is potent to subdue "the attack and menace of every single reptile" (*ibid.*).

It is this supreme angelic being who in one line

of apocalyptic tradition becomes the heavenly Son of Man—a conception that exercised an important influence on Christological development.[1]

Over against Jaoel stands Azazel, who here appears as the arch-fiend,[2] and as active upon the earth (chap. xiii.), though his real domain is in Hades, where he reigns as lord (chap. xxxi.). In fact, according to the peculiar representation of our Apocalypse, Azazel is himself the fire of Hell (cf. chap. xiv. " Be thou the burning coal of the furnace of the earth," and xxxi., " burnt with the fire of Azazel's tongue "). He is the source of all wickedness and uncleanness (chap. xiii.), and the godless are his heritage (*ibid.*). He is denounced as the slanderer of truth and the seducer of mankind, having " scattered over the earth the secrets of heaven," and " rebelled against the Mighty One " (chap. xiv.). The radical dualism of the Book comes out not only in the sharp division of mankind into two hosts, which stand for Jewry and heathendom respectively, but also in the clearly defined contradistinction of two ages, the present Age of ungodliness and the future Age of righteousness (cf. chap. xxix. and ix.). The present Age— called " this æon " (chap. xxxi)—is " corruptible " (chap. xvii.), " the Age of ungodliness " (chap. xxix., xxxii.), during which the heathen have the dominion over the Jews (chap. xxxi.); it is to last " twelve " years or " hours " (chap. xxix.). Over against it stands " the coming Age " (chap. xxxi.), or " Age of the righteous " (chap. xvii., xxix.). The origin of sin is traced to the Fall, which is described in chap. xxiii. The agent is, of course, the serpent, who is merely the instrument of Azazel. Indeed, the twelve wings of the latter are given in the description to the serpent. The evil spirit, who is described as

[1] Cf. *E.A.*, p. 284. The name Jaoel (Yahoel) occurs as the name of a principal angel (over fire) in the Kabbalistic Book *Berith Menuḥa* 57*a*, and below him are seven others, including Gabriel : see Lueken, *Michael*, p. 54.

[2] So in one form of the tradition in 1 Enoch, Azazel stands at the head of the fallen angels.

being "between" the human pair in the Garden, "representeth ungodliness, their beginning (on the way) to perdition, even Azazel," and the seer proceeds to ask why God has given "power to such to destroy the generation of men in their works upon the earth." In some sense, then, according to the representation of our Apocalypse, the sin of Adam affects the destinies of all his descendants. The moral poison of sensuality (Heb. *zôhămā*) with which the serpent infected Eve (T. B., *Yĕbāmôth*, 103 *b*) passed on to all generations (cf. *Wisdom* ii. 24, 4 Ezra iii. 21).[1] This has an important bearing on the Pauline doctrine of original sin. At the same time, our Apocalypse, in spite of its strong expression of predestinarian views elsewhere, insists with marked emphasis upon the freedom of man's will (cf. chap. xxvi.).

The Book apparently knows nothing of a resurrection. The righteous dead, it would seem, proceed straight to the heavenly Paradise ("the Garden of Eden"), where they enjoy heavenly "fruits and blessedness" (chap. xxi.), while the wicked dead go immediately to the underworld and Azazel. Nothing is said of an intermediate state. The more usual view is that the heavenly Paradise is reserved for the righteous dead, who will enter it after the final judgement (except for a few privileged saints like Enoch, who are allowed to enter it beforehand). The nearest parallel to the idea of our Book, seems to occur in 1 Enoch lx. 8, 23, lxi. 12, lxx. 4, where the elect righteous already dwell in the garden of life.

"A judgement" is spoken of "at the end of the

---

[1] In T.B. *Aboda zara* 22*b* R. Joḥanan refers to this as follows: *At the moment when the serpent came upon Eve he infected her with sensuality* (*zôhămā*). Was this also the case with Israel (generally)? *When the Israelites stood upon Mount Sinai their infection* (*impulse to sensuality, zôhămāthān*) *ceased; the aliens* (heathen) *who did not stand upon Mount Sinai—their infection* (of sensuality) *did not cease.* The Covenant on Mount Sinai annulled the effects of the Fall.

world," but it is a judgment upon the heathen nations effected by Israel at the end of the present age of ungodliness [1] (cf. chap. xxii., xxix.).

A detailed eschatological description of the end of the present age of ungodliness and the coming in of the age of righteousness is given in chap. xxix.–xxxi. In chap. xxix. it is stated that before the beginning of the new Age God's judgement will be effected on the ruthless heathen nations by God's people [2]; ten plagues come upon all creatures of the earth on account of sin; those who are of Abraham's seed survive according to a pre-determined number, hasten to Jerusalem, wreak vengeance on their foes, and rejoice before God, to whom they return (chap. xxix.). In the following chapter (xxx.) a detailed description is given of the ten plagues which visit the heathen "at the twelfth hour of the present Age." Chap. xxxi. describes the trumpet-blast which announces the mission of God's Elect One (the Messiah), who gathers together the dispersed of Israel, and the annihilation and horrible doom of the godless foes of Israel and of God's enemies both within and without Israel (the former renegade Jews), and the joy which the downfall of these wicked people and the signal manifestation of God's righteousness cause.

It will be noticed that chaps. xxx. and xxxi. duplicate to some extent the contents of chap. xxix. They read like an appendix. Moreover, the figure of the Messiah first emerges here, and his *rôle* is a somewhat limited one. The last words of chap. xxix. ("And lo! I am with you for ever") may well have formed the conclusion of the Apocalypse.

It should be noted also that in the Christian addition in chap. xxix. no emphasis is laid upon Christ's divinity. The description reads like an Ebionitic one.

---

[1] The "judgement of the Great Assize" mentioned in chap. xxiv. occurs in a clause which is absent from S, and may be an interpolation.

[2] According to chapter xxii. these peoples are destined "some for judgement and restoration, and others for vengeance and destruction at the end of the world."

In this connexion it may be noted that the identification of the fruit of the forbidden tree in chap. xxiii. with the grape may reflect the ascetic tendency, which grew up in Jewish (and Jewish-Christian) circles after the destruction of Jerusalem, to abstain from wine as a mark of mourning. This feeling may have stimulated the view that wine was the source of woe to mankind (see note on passage). Apparently the Essenes regarded Jonadab, the founder of the sect of " water-drinkers " (Rechabites), as a prototype of the Essene order (see *J.E.*, v. 230*b*).

As has been pointed out above, our Apocalypse, like the companion one of *The Ascension of Isaiah*, and other examples in the apocalyptic literature, expresses the mystical tradition and experience associated with the mysteries of the Divine Chariot or Throne. The speculation which gave rise to this tradition starts from Ezekiel's Chariot-Vision (Ezek. i.), and is embodied in a fairly extensive literature especially in i. and ii. Enoch in the earlier Apocalyptic, and in the neo-Hebraic " Hekalot " literature (eighth to tenth centuries A.D.). The material of which it is composed, and which is constantly re-shaped, consists mainly of descriptions of the seven heavens " with their hosts of angels, and the various storehouses of the world, and of the divine throne above the highest heaven."[1] Heaven is pictured as filled with light of inexpressible brilliance, and the Divine Chariot is surrounded by fiery angels of warlike aspect. The mystic who is allowed to enter the celestial sphere usually receives divine disclosures about the future or the spiritual world.

In order to enjoy this experience the mystic has to prepare himself to enter the ecstatic state which is brought about especially by ablutions and fasting, but also sometimes by fervent invocations and by other means. He is rewarded by " the vision of the Merkabah " or " Divine Chariot " (*sĕfiyyath ha-merkābā*). Those who thus imagined themselves entering the Heavenly Chariot and floating through the air were called *Yôrĕdê Merkābā, i.e.* " those

[1] Cf. *J.E.*, viii. 499*b*.

who go down (embark) into the ship-like chariot" (Jellinek). "In this chariot they are supposed to ascend to the heavens, where in the dazzling light surrounding them they behold the innermost secrets of all persons and things otherwise impenetrable and invisible."[1] The heavenly charioteer is Metatron (according to Kohler suggested by Mithra), the angel next the Throne, whose name is like God's, and who possesses all knowledge, and imparts it to man. Metatron, as we have seen, is Enoch transformed. In our Book he seems to appear under the name Jaoel. It is interesting to note that according to the late Jewish "Hekalot" the initiated one who is admitted to the heavenly regions, in order to be allowed to step before the Divine Throne must recite certain prayers until God Himself addresses him, if he be worthy; cf. with this the Hymn-Prayer which Abraham is taught to recite in chap. xvii. of our Book. According to Kohler[2] the Merkabah-mysteries "remained the exclusive property of the initiated ones, the Ṣenû'îm or Ḥashshā'îm," whom he identifies with the Essenes.

[The emphasis that is laid throughout all parts of the Book upon the sin of idolatry is noteworthy, and especially that the Temple-sacrifices had been polluted by idolatrous rites (cf. chap. xxiv.). Perhaps this is intended to suggest a reason why the sanctuary was destroyed.]

Literary Affinities and Special Importance of the Book

Our Apocalypse has affinities, as has already been pointed out, with such books as *The Ascension of Isaiah*, which like it deals with the mysteries of the heavens[2] and is set in a similar mystical framework.

---

[1] Cf. *J.E.*, viii. 499b.

[2] The seven heavens are referred to, and partly described in our Apocalypse in chap. xix. Another point of contact is the reference to the "heavenly garment" in chap. xiii.,

But the latter work has a pronouncedly Christian element, and is a production of Jewish-Christian origin in its present form, whereas in our Book the Christian element is confined to a short interpolated passage in chap. xxix.

With the *Testament of Abraham*, there is a certain affinity, and this work, like our Apocalypse, may be of Essene origin. But the two books are quite distinct, and their historical setting is different. The *Testament*, though it contains an apocalyptic element in the parts which describe Abraham's " ride " through the heavenly regions when he sees the fate of departed souls, is based upon the idea of Abraham's death; moreover, the chief angelic figure in the *Testament* is Michael, and the eschatology is different. Possibly the eschatology of the two Books may be regarded as complementary, the *Apocalypse* giving the national, and the *Testament* the individual aspects of it from the Essene standpoint.

There is, too, a certain affinity with the Clementine literature (*Homilies* and *Recognitions*), which is highly important for the history of Gnostic Judæo-Christianity. Thus in the Clementine *Homilies* the doctrine of contrasts is much elaborated. The ruler of this world is Satan, the ruler of the future world is the Messiah. The divinity of Christ is not recognised, no stress is laid upon the doctrine of the atonement, and strict asceticism is enjoined.

Our Book is important as illustrating the Jewish ideas that lie behind the doctrine of original sin in connexion with the story of the Fall, and in its angelology and demonology. In the angelic figure of Jaoel (= Michael = Metatron), God's vicegerent and the imparter of divine revelation to man (in the person of Abraham) we have one more illustration of the range of conceptions on the Jewish side which

---

end. For a discussion of the theological affinities of these ideas with the New Testament writings cf. Introduction to *The Ascension of Isaiah*, pp. xxi –xxiv.

influenced the Logos-idea and Christological development. The pessimistic estimate of the world as it is—" the æon of ungodliness—which to a large extent is under the dominion of Azazel, illustrates such phrases as " the god of this world " (2 Cor. iv. 4), " the ruler of this world " (John xii. 31) which are applied to Satan. These probably reflect popular Jewish feeling. The earth is the Lord's, as St. Paul himself insists (1 Cor. x. 26), but has fallen under the dominion of the evil one, and can only be redeemed therefrom by God's Messiah.

Our Book is specially important as one more interesting example of the apocalyptic ideas of late Judaism, and, more particularly, as throwing a welcome light on the ideas specially congenial to early Jewish-Christianity when it had already become, to some extent, detached from the common stream of Church life.

BIBLIOGRAPHY

For the editions of the Slavonic text see the second section of this Introduction.

A valuable German translation of the Slavonic text, with critical notes and Introduction, has been published in the series *Studien zur Geschichte der Theologie und Kirche* : it is edited by Prof. G. Nathanael Bonwetsch (Leipzig, 1897).

Articles by Ginzberg in *J.E.*, i. 91 f.; Lagrange in *Revue Biblique*, 1905, pp. 511–514; see also Schürer, *Geschichte des jüdischen Volkes*, iii. pp. 336-338.

SHORT TITLES, ABBREVIATIONS, AND BRACKETS USED IN THIS EDITION

1 Enoch = The Ethiopic Book of Enoch.
2 Enoch = The Slavonic Book of Enoch.
Ap. Bar. = The Syriac Apocalypse of Baruch.
The Greek Apocalypse of Baruch = The Apocalypse edited under this title (and based upon a Greek and also a Slavonic text) by Dr. H. Maldwyn Hughes in the Oxford Corpus of *The Apocrypha and Pseudepigrapha of the Old Testament*, ii. pp. 527-541.

INTRODUCTION xxxiii

Asc. Is. = The Ascension of Isaiah.
Pirke de R. Eliezer is cited according to the edition (English translation and notes) of G. Friedlander (London, 1916).
Beer = *Leben Abraham's nach Auffassung der jüdischen Sage*, von Dr. B. Beer (Leipzig, 1859).
Bonwetsch = *Die Apokalypse Abrahams* . . . herausgegeben von G. Nathanael Bonwetsch (Leipzig, 1897, in the series *Studien zur Geschichte der Theologie und der Kirche*).
Volz = *Jüdische Eschatologie von Daniel bis Akiba*, dangesvellt von Paul Volz (Tübingen und Leipzig, 1903).
Weber = *Jüdische Theologie auf Grund des Talmud und verwandter Schriften:* von Dr. Ferdinand Weber (Leipzig, 1897).
S = Codex Sylvester (first half of fourteenth century) : Facsimile Edition, Petrograd, 1890 (edited also by Tikhonravov).

P = Palæa (Old Testament narratives and expositions in Slavonic).
A = a Palæa-text of *Ap. Abr*, edited by Tikhonravov from a MS. of the fifteenth century.
K = a Palæa-text of *Ap. Abr.*, edited by I. Porfir'ev from a MS. of the seventeenth century.
R = a Palæa-text of *Ap. Abr.*, i.–viii., edited by A. Pypin from a MS. dated 1494.

See further the second section of the Introduction

Luecken = *Michael : eine Darstellung und Vergleichung der jüdischen und der morgenländisch-christlichen Tradition vom Erzengel Michael:* von Wilhelm Luecken (Göttingen, 1898).
E.A. = *The Ezra-Apocalypse*, edited by G. H. Box (1912).
J.Q.R. = Jewish Quarterly Review.
D.B. = Dictionary of the Bible.
J.E. = Jewish Encyclopædia.
M.T. = Masoretic Text.

[ ] Square brackets enclosing words in smaller type indicate additional, and in most cases presumably interpolated, matter, which is absent from S.

( ) Round brackets enclosing words in *italic type* indicate glosses or editorial additions.

( ) Round brackets enclosing words in ordinary type indicate additions to the text of the translation made for the sake of clearness.

For the works cited under the following names—
Tikhonravov, see pp. xi, xiv.
Sreznevsky, see p. xi.
Pypin, see p. xiv.
Porfir'ev, see p. xiv.

[The translation that follows has been prepared with the assistance of Mr. J. I. Landsman, who has consulted
c

for this purpose the Facsimile Edition of Codex S, and the various printed editions referred to above. For the form of the translation here given Mr. Landsman takes full responsibility. No previous translation or edition of the Book has been published in English so far as the Editor is aware.]

THE APOCALYPSE OF ABRAHAM

PART I

The Legend (Chapters I.–VIII.)

Title [1]

The Book of the Revelation of Abraham, the son of Terah, the son of Nahor, the son of Serug, the son of Roog (Reu [2]), the son of Arphaxad, the son of Shem, the son of Noah, the son of Lamech, the son of Methuselah, the son of Enoch, the son of Jared (Arad).

Abraham's Conversion from Idolatry
(Chapters I.–VIII.).

I. On the day when I planed the gods of my father [3] Terah and the gods of Nahor *his brother*,[4] when I was searching as to who the Mighty God in truth is—I, Abraham, at the time when it fell to my lot, when I fulfilled the services (*the sacrifices* [5]) of

---

[1] The whole of the title occurs only in S.

[2] Some links in the genealogical chain are omitted: Reu son of Peleg, son of Eber, son of Shelah, son of Arphaxad (Gen. xi. 10–16); Abraham was thus " the tenth from Noah " (Josephus, *Ant.*, i. 6, 5).

[3] Abraham is represented as having followed the occupation of his father, that of an idol-maker; cf. *Bereshith rabba* on Gen. xi. 28 (see Appendix, p. 90).

[4] *his* (*i. e.* Abraham's) *brother;* probably a gloss (the structure of the narrative demands " my "); A omits.

[5] Probably a gloss (so Tikhonravov); or read *of the altar* for *sacrifices* (Bonwetsch).

my father Terah to his gods of wood and stone, gold
and silver, brass and iron;[1] having entered into their
temple for service, I found the god whose name was
Merumath[2] (which was) hewn out of stone, fallen
forward at the feet of the iron god Nahon.[3] And
it came to pass, when I saw it, my heart was perplexed, and[4] I considered in my mind that I should
not be able to bring him back to his place, I, Abraham,
alone,[5] because he was heavy, being of a large stone,[6]
and I went forth and made it known to my father.
And he entered with me, and when both of us moved
him (the god) forward, so that we might bring him
back[7] to his place, his head fell from him [8] while I
was still holding him by the head. And it came
to pass,[8] when my father saw that the head of
Merumath[9] had fallen from him, he said to me:
"Abraham!" And I said: "Here am I." And
he said to me: "Bring me an axe, of the small
ones,[10] from the house." And I brought it to him.
[11] And he hewed aright another Merumath out of
another stone, without head, and the head which
had been thrown down from Merumath he placed
upon it, and the rest of Merumath he shattered.[11]

II. And he made five other gods, and gave them
to me [and][12] commanded me to sell them outside
in the street of the town. And I saddled my father's[13]

[1] Cf. Dan. v. 4.

[2] The stone idol Merumath (= Heb. *'eben mĕrûmā*, " stone
of deceit ") was the chief object of Abraham's worship at
this period.

[3] So A; S has *Naritson*; K, *by name Nahin*.

[4] *and* omitted by S.

[5] *I Abraham alone*: K omits; S, + *and lo !*

[6] *being of a large stone*: R omits.

[7] *so that we might bring him back*: R omits.

[8-8] R omits.   [9] + *his god*, K.

[10] *of the small ones*: K omits.

[11-11] K reads: *And he cut off the head of another god of stone
and fastened it upon the god Merumath which fell before, and
the head which fell down from him and the rest of the other god
he shattered.*

[12] *and*: S K omit.

[13] *father's*: A omits.

ass, and placed them upon it, and went towards the inn to sell them. And lo! merchants from Fandana [1] in Syria were travelling with camels going to Egypt,[2] to trade.[3] And I spoke with them. And one of their camels uttered a groan, and the ass took fright and sprang away and upset the gods; and three of them were smashed, and two were preserved. And it came to pass, when the Syrians saw that I had gods, they said to me : " Why didst thou not tell us [that thou hadst gods ? Then we would have bought them] [4] before the ass heard the sound of the camel, and they would not have been lost. Give us, at any rate, the gods that remain, and we will give thee the proper price [5] for the broken gods, also for the gods that have been preserved." [5] For I was concerned in my heart as to how I could bring to my father the purchase-price ; [6] and the three broken ones I cast into the water of the river Gur, which was at that place, and they sank into the depths,[7] and there was nothing more of them.

III. When I was still going on the way, my heart was perplexed within me, and my mind was distracted. And I said in my heart : [" What evil deed is this that my father is doing ? Is not he, rather, the god of his gods, since they come into existence through his chisels and lathes, and his wisdom, and is it not rather fitting that they should worship my father, since they are his work ? What is this delusion of my father in his works ?][8] Behold, Merumath fell and could not rise in his own temple, nor could I, by myself, move him until my father came, and the two of us moved him ; and as we were thus too weak, his

[1] *Fandana* probably = Paddan-Aram (Gen. xxv. 20).

[2] Cf. Gen. xxxvii. 25.

[3] K reads : *in order to buy from thence papyrus from the Nile. And I questioned them, and they informed me.*

[4] S omits.

[5-5] A K omit; they read instead: *And I deliberated in my heart, and they gave me the value.*

[6] K reads : *and he took the pieces of the broken gods and cast them in the Dead Sea, from which it could never emerge.*

[7] A K, + *of the river Gur.*

[8] This passage is given by A K, but is absent from S; apparently it is a later interpolation

head fell from him, and he (*i.e.* my father) set it upon another stone of another god,[1] which he had made without head. And the other five gods were broken in pieces down from the ass, which were able neither to help themselves,[2] nor to hurt the ass, because [3] it had broken them to pieces; nor did their broken fragments come up out of the river."[4] And I said in my heart: "If this be so, how can Merumath, my father's god, having the head of another stone, [5]and himself being made of another stone,[5] rescue a man, or hear a man's prayer and reward him?"[6]

IV. And while I cogitated thus, I reached my father's house; and having watered the ass, and set out hay for it, I brought the silver and gave it into the hand of my father Terah. When he saw it he was glad, [and][7] he said: "Blessed art thou, Abraham, of my gods,[8] because thou hast brought the price of the gods, so that my work was not in vain." And I answered and said to him: "Hear, O my father, Terah! Blessed are the gods [9]of thee, for thou art their god, since [9] thou hast made them; for their blessing is ruination, and their power [10] is vain;[11] they who did not help themselves,[12] how shall they, then, help thee or bless me [13]? I have been

---

[1] Cf. *Wisdom* xiii. 10 ("a useless stone, the work of an ancient hand"); K reads: *and set upon him the stone head of another god*.

[2] Cf. *Wisdom* xiii. 16 ("knowing that it is unable to help itself").

[3] = ? *although* (Heb. *'aph ki*; Rabbinic *'aph 'al pi*).

[4] According to the Mishna '*Abôdā zārā* iii. 3 it was the duty of Jews to destroy an idol by sinking it in the waters of the Dead Sea, from which it could never emerge.

[5-5] Omitted by K.

[6] Cf. *Wisdom* xiii. 17 f. (the whole chapter should be compared in this context).

[7] S omits.

[8] Lit. *to my gods*: read ? *of* (*by*) *my god* (Bonwetsch).

[9-9] Text of S here corrupt.

[10] A, *help*.

[11] K, powerless.

[12] Cf. note [2] in previous chapter.

[13] For the thought cf. Heb. vii. 7.

kind to thee in this affair,[1] because by (using) my intelligence, I have brought thee the money for the broken gods." And when he heard my [2] word, he became furiously angry with me, because I had spoken hard words against his gods.

V. I, however, having thought over my father's anger, went out; [and after I had gone out] [3] my father [4] cried, saying: "Abraham!" And I said: "Here am I." And he said: "Take and collect the splinters of the wood out of which I made gods of pine-wood before thou camest; and make ready for me the food of the mid-day meal." [5] And it came to pass, when I collected the splinters of wood, I found under them a little god which had been lying among the brush-wood on my left, and on his forehead was written: GOD BARISAT.[6] And [7] I did not inform my father that I had found the wooden god Barisat under the chips. And it came to pass, when I had laid the splinters in the fire, in order that I might make ready food for my father—on going out to ask a question regarding the food, I placed Barisat before the kindled fire,[8] saying threateningly to him: "Pay careful attention, Barisat, [that] [9] the fire do not die down until I come; if, however, it dieth down, blow on it that it may burn up again." And I went out and accomplished my purpose.[10] And on returning I found Barisat fallen backwards, and [11] his feet surrounded by fire and horribly burnt.[12] I burst into a fit of laughter, and I said to myself: "Truly, O Barisat, thou

---

[1] Lit. *transaction*.   [2] K, *this*.
[3] S omits.   [4] S, *he*.
[5] Cf. Is. xliv. 15, *Wisdom* xiii. 12 f.
[6] *Barisat* = probably *bar 'ishtā*, "son of the fire."
[7] A K, + *it came to pass, when I found him, I kept him and*.
[8] Lit. *kindling of the fire*.   [9] S omits.
[10] Lit. *did my counsel*: a Hebrew phrase, *'āsā 'ēṣā*, "execute a plan" (Is. xxx. 1).
[11] S, + *before*.
[12] A, + *And it came to pass when I saw it*,

canst kindle the fire and cook food!" And it came to pass, while I spake (thus) in my laughter [1] he (*i.e.* Barisat) was gradually burnt up by the fire and reduced [2] to ashes. And I brought the food to my father, and he did eat. And I gave him wine and milk,[3] and he was gladdened and blessed his god Merumath. And I said to him: "O father Terah, bless not thy god Merumath, and praise him not, but rather praise thy god Barisat because, loving thee more, he hath cast himself into the fire to cook thy food!" And he said to me: "And where is he now?" [And I said:] [4] "He is burnt to ashes in the violence of the fire and is reduced to dust." And he said: "Great is the power of Barisat! I (will) make another to-day, and to-morrow he will prepare [5] my food."

VI. When I, Abraham, however, heard such words from my father, I laughed in my mind and sighed in the grief and in the anger of my soul, and said: [6] "How then can that which is made by him—manufactured statues—be a helper of my father? Or shall the body then be subject to its soul, and the soul to the spirit, and the spirit to folly and ignorance!" [7] And I said: [6] "It is fitting once to endure evil. So I will direct my mind to what is pure and lay my thoughts open before him." [And] [8] I answered and said: "O father Terah, whichever of these thou praisest as a god, thou art foolish in thy mind. Behold the gods of thy brother

[1] A, *mind*; K, *in my mind and laughed*.

[2] Lit. *became*.

[3] Wine was sometimes mixed not only with water, but with milk, in Palestine; cf. *Cant.* V. 1 (*I have drunk my wine with my milk*); cf. also Is. lv. 1.

[4] S A omit.

[5] Lit. *make*.

[6] *i.e.* thought ("said in my heart"). The sentence that follows ("It is fitting once to endure evil") means: "It is well to suffer in this way for a good cause."

[7] In this sentence the text of S is not in order, and has been corrected by Tikhonravov in accordance with A and K.

[8] Omitted by S.

Ora,[1] which stand in the holy temple, are more worthy of honour than [these of][2] thine. For behold Zucheus, the god of thy brother Oron,[3] is more worthy of honour than thy god Merumath, because he is made of gold which is highly valued by people, and when he groweth old in years he will be re-modelled; but if your god Merumath is changed or broken, he will not be renewed, because he is a stone; the which is also the case with the god Joavon[4] [5][who standeth with Zucheus over the other gods—how[6] much more worthy of honour is he than the god Barisat, who is made of wood, while he is forged of silver! How[6] is he made, by adaptation of man, valuable to outward appearance! But thy god Barisat, while he was still, before he had been prepared, rooted up (?)[7] upon the earth and was great and wonderful with the glory of branches and blossom,[8] thou didst hew out with the axe, and by means of thy art he hath been made into a god. And lo! his fatness is already withered and perished, he is fallen from the height to the ground, he hath come from great estate to littleness, and the appearance of his countenance hath vanished, and he] Barisat himself is burnt up by fire and reduced to ashes and is no more; and thou sayest: "To-day I will make another which [9] to-morrow shall make ready my food!" [10] "He hath perished to utter destruction!"[10]

VII. [11] "Behold, the fire is more worthy of honour

---

[1] *i.e.* Haran (so S); A has *thy father Nahor*, K *my brother Nahor*. [2] Omitted by S.

[3] Another form of Haran (so S); A and K read as indicated in the previous note.

[4] So S: A, *Joauv*; K, *Joav*; R, *Jav*.

[5] The long passage in brackets which here follows is extant in A and K, but is wanting in S. It consists of a long comparison between the gods Joauv (Joavon) and Barisat, and is very obscure. It is probably a later interpolation.

[6] Lit. *that*. [7] ? read *rooted*.

[8] *i.e.* while it was growing as a tree. [9] Lit. *and he*.

[10,10] *Hath he not abandoned this (once for all) by perishing to utter destruction?* A (K).

[11] A K insert at the beginning of this chapter: *Having thought thus, Abraham came to his father, saying: " Father Terah,"* forgetting that Abraham was already speaking to him. The sentence is wanting in S.

than ¹ all things formed because even that which is not subjected is subjected unto it, and things easily perishable are mocked by its flames.¹ ² But even more worthy of honour is the water,² because it conquereth the fire and ³ satisfieth the earth.³ But even it I do not call God, because ⁴ it is subjected to the earth under which the water inclineth.⁴ But I call the earth much more worthy of honour, because it overpowereth the nature (*and the fulness*) ⁵ of the water. Even it (viz. the earth), however, I do not call god, [because] ⁶ it, too, is dried up by the sun, [and] ⁶ is apportioned to man to be tilled.⁷ [I call the sun more worthy of honour than the earth,] ⁸ because it with its rays illumineth the whole world ⁹ and the different atmospheres.⁹ [But] ⁶ even it I do not call god, because at night ¹⁰ and by clouds its course is obscured.¹⁰ Nor, again, do I call the moon or the stars god, because they also in their season obscure [their] ¹¹ light at night.¹² [But] ¹¹ hear [this],¹¹ Terah my father; for ¹³ I will make known to thee ¹³ the God who hath made everything, not these we consider as gods. Who then is He? or what is He?

Who hath crimsoned the heavens, and made the
  sun golden,

¹·¹ So S; for this A K have *thy honoured gods of gold, silver, stone, and wood, because it burneth up thy gods; yea, thy gods are burnt up in subjection to the fire, while the fire mocked them, devouring thy gods.*

²·² A K read: *But that* (viz. the fire) *I do not call god, because it hath been subjected to the water, while the water is more worthy of honour than it* (*i. e.* the fire).

³·³ A K, *maketh the fruits of the earth sweet.*

⁴·⁴ A K, *the water inclineth under the earth.*

⁵ So S; but A K omit—it is probably a gloss.

⁶ S omits. ⁷ Lit. *for work* (= Heb. *la'ăbōd*).

⁸ Omitted by S; but it must have belonged to the original text. It is attested by A K.

⁹·⁹ So S; A K omit: *atmospheres* (? lower and upper) = 'ἀέρες; cf. 4 Ezra vi. 4, *altitudines aerum.*

¹⁰·¹⁰ A K, *it is obscured by the darkness.*

¹¹ S omits. ¹² Or *by* (*through*) *night.*

¹³·¹³ Lit. *I will investigate* (or *examine*) *before thee concerning.* The question that follows, *Who then is He?* etc., gives the subject of the investigation.

And the moon lustrous, and with it the stars;
And hath made the earth dry in the midst of many
    waters,
    And set thee in [1] . . . . [2][and tested me in the
        confusion of my thoughts][2]
" Yet may God reveal Himself to us through
Himself ! "

VIII. And it came to pass while I spake [3] thus to
my father Terah in the court of my [4] house, there
cometh down [5] the voice of a Mighty One [6] from
heaven in a fiery cloud-burst,[7] saying and crying:
" Abraham, Abraham ! " And I said : " Here am
I." And He said : [8] " Thou art seeking in the understanding of thine heart the God of Gods and the
Creator ; [8] [9] I am He : [9] Go out from thy father
Terah, and get thee out from the [10] house, that thou
also be not slain in the sins of thy father's house."
And I went out. And it came to pass when I went
out, that before I succeeded in getting out in front
of the door of the court, there came a sound of a
[great] [11] thunder [12] and burnt [13] him and [13] his
house,[13] and everything whatsoever in his house,
down to the ground, forty cubits.[14]

[1] Something has to be supplied here.
[2][2] So A K; S omits.   [3] S K, *reflected*.
[4] A K, *his* (*i.e.* Terah's), rightly. At this point there
follows in A K (R) an insertion which contains, among
other things, a version of the well-known legend about
Abraham's burning of the idol-temple, and with it his brother
Haran; cf. Appendix I.
[5] Lit. *falleth* (S); K, *fell* (A omits).
[6] = LXX. ὁ ἰσχυρός (frequent as a rendering of Heb.
hā'ēl, " God "); cf. 4 Ezra ix. 45, etc.   [7] K, *flame*.
[8][8] The text of S is not in order; Sreznevsky reads :
Cogu Coisya, God thou dost fear, and the Creator thou art seeking.
[9][9] A omits.   [10] K, *his*.   [11] S omits.
[12] K, + *and there fell fire from heaven*.
[13][13] A (K R) omit.
[13] K, + *and the dwellers therein, both men and beasts*.
[14] Here R ends. The Midrashic story about the burning
of Terah's house is really based upon an interpretation of
the Biblical " Ur of the Chaldees " (Gen. xi. 31, xv. 7).
Here " Ur " is interpreted as = " fire "; Abraham was
brought out of " Ur " (" fire ") by the Lord.

PART II

The Apocalypse (Chapters IX.-XXXII.).

Abraham receives a Divine Command to offer Sacrifice after Forty Days as a Preparation for a Divine Revelation (Chapter IX.; cf. Gen. xv.).

IX. Then a voice came to me speaking twice: "Abraham, Abraham!" And I said: "Here am I!" And He said: "Behold, [1] it is I [1]; *fear not*,[2] for I am before the worlds,[3] and a mighty God who hath created [4] the light of the world.[4] *I am a shield over thee*,[2] and I am thy helper. Go, take me *a young heifer of three years old, and a she-goat of three years old, and a ram of three years old, and a turtledove and a pigeon*,[5] and bring me a pure sacrifice. And in this sacrifice I will lay before thee the ages (to come), and make known to thee what is reserved, and thou shalt see great things which thou hast not seen (hitherto); [6]

[1-1] K, *I am with thee.*   [2] Cf. Gen. xv. 1.

[3] Or *ages* ("æons").

[4-4] A, *the first light;* K, *in the beginning heaven and earth and then the first luminary of light and of the world* (cf. Gen. i. 1 f.). The reference is apparently to the created (not the uncreated) light. For the latter cf. note on chap. xvii.

[5] Cf. Gen. xv. 9.

[6] The revelation made to Abraham which is described in Gen. xv. 9 f. early became a favourite theme for apocalyptic speculation, and an intimation was discovered in the passage of Israel's later captivity and subjection to the four oppressive world-powers of the Book of Daniel (see the Targums *ad loc.*). This apocalyptic experience of Abraham is referred to in 4 Ezra iii. 14 (*and unto him* [Abraham] *only didst thou reveal the end of the times secretly by night*). According to the *Ap. Bar.* iv. 4 the heavenly Jerusalem was shown to Abraham "by night among the portions of the victims."

because thou hast loved to search me out, and I have named thee my Friend.[1] But abstain [2] from every form of food that proceedeth out of the fire, and from the drinking of wine, and from anointing (thyself) with oil, forty days,"[3] and then set forth for me the sacrifice which I have commanded thee, in the place *which I will shew thee, on a high mountain*,[4] and there I will shew thee the ages which have been created and established, [5] made and renewed,[5] by my Word,[6] and [7] I will make known to thee what shall come to pass in them on those who have done evil and (practised) righteousness in the generation of men.

Abraham, under the Direction of the Angel Jaoel, proceeds to Mount Horeb, a Journey of Forty Days, to offer the Sacrifice (Chapters X.–XII.).

X. And it came to pass, when I heard the voice of Him who spake such words to me, (and) [8] I looked hither and thither and lo! there was no breath of a

---

[1] Or "lover." Abraham, as God's chosen friend (or "lover of God," cf. 2 Chron. xx. 7, Is. xli. 8, Ep. James ii. 23) can receive special revelation; for the juxtaposition of the two ideas cf. 4 Ezra iii. 14.

[2] Or *refrain thyself*. By *every form of food that proceedeth out of the fire*, flesh-meat is no doubt meant.

[3] Fasting as a preparation for the reception of a divine revelation was much practised by the apocalyptists. In 4 Ezra four fasts of seven days followed in each case by a divine revelation are referred to. Here, it is to be noted, the period is one of forty days. For the terms here used cf. 4 Ezra ix. 24. Anointing the body (especially the face) with oil was a mark of joy used in connexion with feasting (cf. Eccles. ix. 8, Ps. xxiii. 5, Amos vi. 6), and omitted in mourning as a sign of grief (cf. 2 Sam. xiv. 2, Dan. x. 3).

[4] Cf. Gen. xxii. 2.

[5 5] A omits.

[6] The "Word" of God here has a quasi-personal significance; cf. 4 Ezra vi. 38 ("and thy Word, O Lord, perfected the work"), 43, etc.

[7] *and* omitted by A.

[8] Omit (a Hebraism? marks apodosis).

man,[1] [2] and my spirit was affrighted, and my soul fled from me, and I became like a stone, and fell down upon the earth, for [2] I had no more strength to stand on the earth.[3] [4] And while I was still lying with my face upon the earth,[4] I heard the voice of the Holy One speaking : " Go, Jaoel,[5] and by means of my ineffable Name raise me yonder man, and strengthen him (so that he recover) from his trembling." And the angel came, whom He had sent to me, in the likeness of a man, and [6] grasped me by my right hand, and set me up upon my feet, and said to me : [7] " [8] Stand up,[8] [Abraham,] [9] Friend of God who loveth thee; let not [10] the trembling of man seize thee ! For, lo ! I have been sent to thee to strengthen thee and bless thee in the name of God—who loveth thee—the Creator of the celestial and terrestrial. Be fearless and hasten to Him. I am called Jaoel [11] by Him who moveth that which existeth with me on the

---

[1] Cf. 4 Ezra vii. 29 (" omnes qui spiramentum habent hominis ").

[2-2] K reads : *and he was affrighted in his spirit, and his soul perished in him, and he became like a dead man, and fell down like a stone upon the earth, and.*

[3] Cf. Ezek. i. 28; Dan. viii. 17, x. 8 f.; 1 Enoch xiv. 14, 24; 4 Ezra x. 29 f.

[4-4] K omits.

[5] The name of the archangel Joel (Jaoel) is differently spelt in the various texts (cf. the Slavonic version of *The Book of Adam*, ed. by Jagić, in *Denkschriften des Kaiserlichen Akademie der Wissenschaften in Wien, philol.-histor. Classe*, Vol. XLII.) : S, *Naoil, Iloil ;* A, *Aol,* K, *Jaol, Book of Adam, Joil* = *Joel. Jaoel* (= Heb. *Yahoel*) is represented in our Apocalypse as a being possessed of the power of the ineffable name, a function assigned in the Rabbinical writings to Metatron, " whose name is like unto that of God Himself " (T.B. *Sanh.* 38b). The name *Yahoel* (Jaoel) is evidently a substitute for the ineffable name *Yahweh*, the writing out of which in full was forbidden. In chap. xvii. below God Himself is addressed as *Jaoel.* For Jaoel as the heavenly choirmaster cf. note on chap. xvii.

[6] A omits.

[7] Cf. 4 Ezra x. 30.

[8-8] A omits.

[9] S omits.

[10] A K, *if.*

[11] S, *Eloel ;* A, *Aol ;* K, *Ioal.*

seventh[1] expanse upon[2] the firmament,[3] a power in virtue of the ineffable Name that is dwelling in me.[4] I am the one who hath been given to restrain, according to His commandment, the threatening attack of the living creatures of the Cherubim against one another,[5] and teach those who carry Him[6] the song of the seventh hour of the night of man.[7] I am ordained to restrain the Leviathan, for unto me are subject the attack and menace of every single reptile.[8] [I am he who hath been commissioned to loosen

[1] A, *middle*.   [2] *i.e.* ? " over."
[3] The angel sent to Isaiah to conduct him through the various " heavens " had " come from the seventh [*i.e.* the highest] heaven "; cf. *Asc. Is.* vi. 13, vii. 27.
[4] Cf. Ex. xxiii. 21 (" my name is in him," *i.e.* the angel of Jahveh); here Jaoel seems to play the *rôle* of Michael (see Introduction, p. xxv).
[5] By " the living creatures of the Cherubim " are meant the " holy *ḥayyoth* " of Ezek. i. who are expressly identified with the [heavenly] Cherubim in Ezek. x. 20. They are four in number (each with four faces), and are the bearers of the divine throne (see next note). Apparently they are here represented as of threatening aspect and in danger of menacing attack upon one another, so that a restraining influence was necessary. According to the Midrash (*Exodus rabba* v.) envy and mistrust are absent from the angelic world, though the angels envied Israel the possession of the Law; but cf. *Asc. Is.* vii. 9.
[6] *i.e.* " the holy *ḥayyoth* [' living creatures '] who carry the throne of glory " (*Sifra* on Lev. i. 1).
[7] According to T.B. *Abôdā zārā* 3*b*, " God sits [at night] and listens to the song of the living creatures [*ḥayyoth*], as it is said (Ps. xlii. 8) : *By day the Lord commandeth His loving-kindness* [*i.e.* judges and sustains the world, and occupies Himself in the study of the Law], *and in the night His song is with me.*" In T.B. *Ḥag.* 12*b* it is said that the companies of ministering angels in the fifth heaven " utter His song in the night, and are silent in the day for the sake of the glory of Israel." In *Pirḳe de R. Elie:er* iv. Michael is represented as the head of the first of four bands of ministering angels who utter praise before the Holy One; cf. also *Mekilta* to Ex. xv. 1; and in the New Testament Luke ii. 13 (the angelic song at night).
[8] Michael is represented in Ḳabbalistic literature as the angel-prince who is set over the element of water (cf. Lueken, *Michael*, p. 54); this conception is probably old, for on it rests the haggadic story that when Solomon married Pharaoh's

Hades, to destroy him who stareth at the dead.]¹ I am the one who was commissioned to set on fire thy father's house together with him, because he displayed reverence for dead (idols).² I have been

---

daughter, Michael drove into the bed of the sea a stick, around which slime gathered, and on which Rome was ultimately built (*Midrash rabba* on Cant. i. 6, in the name of R. Levi, end of third century A.D.). Michael is also the prince of snow, which belongs to the element of water (*Deut. rabba* v. 12). Leviathan as the sea-monster *par excellence* would be subject to him, with all reptiles, though the task of slaying the monster is assigned, by Jewish legend, to Gabriel; but Michael and Gabriel are often confused in these connexions. [For the " spirit of the sea " that restrains it cf. 1 Enoch lx. 16.] The representation here is parallel in a sense with that which depicts Michael as the enemy and conqueror of Satan (cf. Rev. xii. 7 ff.) and in later Christian tradition as the vanquisher of the dragon (cf. Lueken, *op. cit.*, pp. 106 ff.). It should be noted that according to the Kabbalistic book *Raziel* fol. 4a the name of Michael is a powerful charm against the reptiles (cf. Lueken, p. 28).

¹ The bracketed clause is omitted by S. One of Michael's functions (with Gabriel) is to open the gates of Hell and release the sinners therein; see *Yalqut Shim.* on Is. xxvi. 2, and cf. Lueken, *op. cit.*, p. 52. What is meant by " destroying " *him who stareth at the dead* is not clear. It might conceivably refer to the duty of burying the dead. To allow a corpse—even an enemy's—to remain unburied was considered an impiety (cf. Ps. lxxix. 2 f.; Tobit i. 17, ii. 7; Josephus, *Apion*, ii. 29), and it is notable that, according to *The Life of Adam and Eve*, xlviii. 4 f.; (cf. Charles, *Corpus* ii. 151), Michael and Uriel bury the bodies of Adam and Abel in Paradise. But the language of the phrase here hardly suits this. In view of the next clause, where " dead " = dead idols, the reference may perhaps be to idol-worship. In a Byzantine text the story of Michael's contest with the devil about the body of Moses is given a somewhat similar motive. The devil is represented as seeking to bring down Moses' dead body to the Israelites in order that they may worship it—and this may depend originally upon a Jewish source which in this way protested against the Christian worship of saints and relics (cf. Lueken, *op. cit.*, p. 121 f.). But perhaps *stareth at* should be altered to *terrifieth*, and the reference is to Death personified; cf. Add. Note, p. 86 f.

² In the Rabbinical form of the legend (see Appendix) Abraham is rescued from the fiery oven into which he had been cast by Nimrod by Michael, according to the opinion

sent to bless thee now, and the land¹ which the Eternal One, whom thou hast invoked, hath prepared for thee, and for thy sake have I wended my way upon the earth.² Stand up, Abraham! Go without fear; be right glad and rejoice; and I am with thee! For eternal honour hath been prepared for thee by the Eternal One. Go, fulfil the sacrifices commanded. For lo! I have been appointed to be with thee and with the generation prepared (to spring) from thee; and with me Michael³ blesseth thee for ever. Be of good cheer, go!"

XI. And I rose up and saw him who had grasped me by my right hand and set me up upon my feet: and the appearance of his body⁴ was like sapphire, and the look of his countenance like chrysolite, and *the hair of his head like snow,* and the turban upon his head⁵ like the appearance of the rainbow, and the clothing of his garments like purple; and a golden sceptre was in his right hand.⁶ And he said to me:

---

of Eliezer b. Jacob (*Genesis rabba* xliv. 16). Michael, according to the Rabbis, was the defender of the Patriarchs. Strictly it is Gabriel who is the prince of fire.

¹ *i. e.* the land of Palestine. In Mohammedan tradition Michael is the good angel who brings peace and plenty.

² It was Michael who, according to Rabbinic tradition, at various times appeared to Abraham, *e. g.* he told Abraham that Lot had escaped, protected Sarah from being defiled by Abimelech (*Pirḳe de R. Eliezer* xxvi.), announced to Sarah that she should have a son (Gen. xviii. 10), rescued Lot from Sodom (T.B. *Baba meṣia,* 86*b*), and prevented Isaac from being sacrificed by substituting a ram. In *The Test. of Abraham* (i.) it is Michael who comes down and visits Abraham in order to take his soul.

³ Here Michael is associated with the speaker, the archangel Jaoel. This rather suggests that the latter is really fulfilling the *rôle* of Metatron (Michael and Metatron are companions, *Zohar* i. 149*b*). But Jaoel really combines the functions of both. The writer wishes to make it clear that Jaoel is closely associated with Michael.

⁴ K, + *his feet* (a gloss? suggested by Rev. i. 15).

⁵ Cf. Rev. xix. 12 (" upon his head many diadems ").

⁶ Cf. Rev. i. 16 (" and he had in his right hand seven stars "). There is a general resemblance here to the description of the exalted Christ in Rev. i. 14–16, but the details

"Abraham!" And I said: "Here am I, thy servant." And he said: "Let not my look affright thee, nor my speech, that thy soul be not perturbed.[1] Come with me and I will go with thee, until the sacrifice, visible, but after the sacrifice,[2] invisible for ever. Be of good cheer, and come!"

XII. And we went, the two of us together, forty days and nights,[3] and I ate no bread, and drank no water, because my food [4] was to see the angel who was with me, and his speech—that was my drink.[5] And we came to the Mount of God, the glorious Horeb. And I said to the angel: "Singer of the Eternal One! Lo! I have no sacrifice with me,[6] nor am I aware of a place of an altar on the mountain: how can I bring a sacrifice?" And he said to me: "Look round!"[7] [8] And I looked round,[8] and lo! there were following us all the prescribed sacrificial (animals) —the young heifer, and the she-goat, and the ram, and the turtle-dove, and the pigeon.[9] And the angel said to me: "Abraham!" I said: "Here am I."

---

are different except that both have the characteristic descriptive phrase, derived from Dan. vii. 9 ("the hair of his head like pure wool," here "like snow," cf. Rev. i. 14); cf. also 2 Enoch i. 5 (the description of the two angels who visit Enoch). The figure described is regal (notice the purple garments and the sceptre), and is invested with the divine glory; cf. Ezek. i. 26 f.

[1] Or "troubled"; cf. 2 Enoch i. 8, and often in apocalyptic writings.

[2] K, + *I will be*. The angel appears in visible form for the time being. So Michael appears to Abraham "like a very comely warrior" (*Test. Abrah.* i.).

[3] Cf. 1 Kings xix. 8.   [4] S, + *and my drink*.

[5] Cf. John iv. 31–34. Elijah ate and drank before starting on his journey to Horeb, and "went in the strength of that meat forty days and forty nights" (1 Kings xix. 8); cf. Ex. xxiv. 18. There is a close parallel to our text in Philo, *Life of Moses*, Bk. III. 1, where it is said of Moses in the Mount: "he neglected all meat and drink for forty days together, evidently because he had more excellent food than that in those contemplations with which he was inspired from above from heaven."

[6] Cf. Gen. xxii. 7.   [7] A, *behind*.
[8-8] A K omit.   [9] Cf. Gen. xv. 9.

And he said to me : " All these slaughter, and divide the animals *into halves, one against the other*, but the birds do not sever;[1] and (" but ") give to the men, whom I will shew thee, standing by thee, for these are the altar[2] upon the Mountain, to offer a sacrifice to the Eternal; but the turtledove and the pigeon give to me, for I will ascend upon the wings of the bird,[3] in order to shew thee in heaven, and on the earth, and in the sea, and in the abyss, and in the under-world, and in the Garden of Eden, and in its rivers and in the fulness of the whole world and its circle—thou shalt gaze in (them) all. "[4]

Abraham accomplishes the Sacrifice, under the Guidance of the Angel, and refuses to be diverted from his Purpose by Azazel (Chapters XIII.–XIV.).

XIII. And I did everything according to the commandment of the angel, and gave the angels, who had come to us, the divided animals, but the angel[5] took the birds. And I waited for the evening sacrifice. And there flew an unclean bird *down upon the carcasses*,[6] and I drove it away. And the unclean bird spake to me, and said : " What doest thou, Abraham, upon the holy Heights, where no man eateth or

[1] Cf. Gen. xv. 10.

[2] Living men (or rather angels) take the place of the material altar; cf. the metaphorical use of " temple " as applied to the body (cf. John ii. 21; 1 Cor. iii. 16, vi. 19). But such a use of the term " altar " does not appear to have become current in Jewish literature.

[3] The ascent to heaven is accomplished on the wings of a dove. The dove is appropriate in this connexion because of its swiftness (cf. Ps. lv. (6) 7, " Oh that I had wings like a dove," etc.; cf. also Virgil, *Æn.* vi. 190 ff.), and its purity. For the symbolism of the dove applied to Israel, and also to the Holy Spirit (Matt. iii. 16), cf. I. Abrahams, *Studies in Pharisaism and the Gospels*, pp. 47 ff.

[4] The revelations here promised to Abraham correspond to the earlier models given in 1 and 2 Enoch.

[5] K, + *Jaoel.*

[6] Cf. Gen. xv. 11.

drinketh,[1] neither is there upon them (any) food of man, but these [2] consume everything with fire, and (will) burn thee up. [3] Forsake the man, who is with thee, and flee; for if thou ascendest to the Heights they will make an end of thee.[3] And it came to pass, when I saw the bird speak, I said to the angel: " What is this, my lord ? " And he said : " This is ungodliness,[4] this is Azazel." [5] And he said to it : " Disgrace upon thee, Azazel ! For Abraham's lot is in heaven, but thine upon the earth. Because thou hast chosen and loved this for the dwelling-(place) of thine uncleanness, therefore the eternal mighty Lord made thee a dweller upon the earth [6] and through thee every evil spirit of lies,[7] and through

---

[1] *i. e.* they are in the domain of the spiritual sphere, where there is no eating and drinking; cf. *Test. Abrah.* (A) iv., " all the heavenly spirits are incorporeal, and neither eat nor drink."

[2] *i. e.* the heavenly beings.

[3][3] Omitted by A K.

[4] Cf. Zech. v. 8.

[5] Azazel is the fallen archangel, the seducer of mankind, who here, as in the Book of Enoch, fills the *rôle* of Satan or Sammael. He is essentially the spirit of uncleanness, and, in this character, is depicted in our text as descending in the form of an unclean bird. It is interesting to note that the Palestinian Targum on Gen. xv. 11 interprets the unclean birds figuratively of idolatrous peoples (" And there came down idolatrous peoples which are like to unclean birds, to steal away the sacrifices of Israel; but the righteousness of Abram was a shield over them ").

[6] Azazel, who is here clearly a fallen archangel like the later Satan (cf. Bousset, *Relig. d. Judentums*[2], 386), has been expelled from heaven by God. According to 2 Enoch xxix. 5 Satan's domain, after his expulsion, was the air (cf. Eph. ii. 2), but here Azazel is a " dweller upon the earth," where he controls the evil powers (cf. John xii. 31, " prince of this world," Matt. iv. 8 f.). In *The Testaments of the Twelve Patriarchs* (cf. also *Asc. Is.*) Beliar is the arch-fiend, the head of the evil spirits, and the source of impurity and lying. But Azazel, like all celestial beings, can fly through the air (*Gen. rabba* xix.) and assume any form, such as that of a bird (*T. B. Sanh.*, 107a).

[7] Azazel's expulsion carried with it that of his hosts, of which he was the leader. [Note that in chap. xxxi. of our Book Azazel is depicted as the lord of hell.]

thee wrath and trials for the generations of ungodly men;[1] for God, the Eternal, Mighty One, hath not permitted that the bodies of the righteous should be in thy hand,[2] in order that thereby the life of the righteous and the destruction of the unclean may be assured.[3] Hear, friend,[4] begone with shame from me. For it hath not been given to thee to play the tempter in regard to all the righteous. Depart from this man! Thou canst not lead him astray, because he is an enemy to thee, and of those who follow thee and love what thou willest. For, behold, the vesture which in heaven was formerly thine hath been set aside for him,[5] and the mortality which was his hath been transferred to thee." [6]

XIV. The angel said to me: [7] [" Abraham!" And

[1] For the sin and misery brought upon the earth by the fallen angels cf. 1 Enoch viii. 2, ix. 6, 8, x. 7 f., etc.

[2] According to *T.B. Baba bathra*, 17a the "evil impulse" (*yeṣer hā-ra'*) had no power over the three righteous men, Abraham, Isaac, and Jacob. In *The Test. Abrah.* Abraham is represented as sinless.

[3] Notice the strong dualism. The activity of the evil powers makes perdition certain for their victims, while, on the other hand, by its very failure in the case of the righteous it makes their felicity more certain in the end.

[4] [Lit. "counsellor," an idiomatic expression still found in Russian dialects (cf. Dalj's *Dictionary of the Russian Language*, s.v. *sovetnik*) meaning "friend," used in a good-humoured way.—J. I. L.]

[5] The "heavenly garments" are here referred to "which are now stored up on high in the seventh heaven" according to *Asc. Is.* iv. 16. The idea, originally a realistic one, was gradually spiritualised, and came to mean the spiritual bodies in which the righteous will be clothed in heaven; cf. 1 Enoch lxii. 15 f. ("garments of glory," "garments of life"); cf. also 2 Enoch xxii. 8 f., where Michael is bidden by God to "take from Enoch his earthly robe . . . and clothe him with the garment of my glory." In *The Ascension of Isaiah* the seer is unable to ascend to the highest heaven until his "garment" has been brought to him (*Asc. Is.* ix. 1-2). There he sees the crowns and garments which are reserved for the righteous (*ibid.* ix. 13 ff.); cf. also *Asc. Is.* viii. 14; Rev. iii. 4, 5, 18, vi. 11, vii. 9; 2 Cor. v. 3 ff.

[6] Azazel has thus lost his "garment of life," or robe of immortality, and become mortal, while Abraham gains it.

[7] S, *Abraham*.

I said: "Here am I, thy servant." And he said: "Know from henceforth that the Eternal One hath chosen thee, (He) whom thou lovest; be of good courage and use this authority, so far as I bid thee, against him who slandereth truth;[1] should I not be able to put him to shame who hath scattered over the earth the secrets of heaven[2] and hath rebelled[3] against the Mighty One?⁴]⁵ Say to him: 'Be thou the burning coal of the Furnace of the earth;[6] go, Azazel, into the inaccessible parts of the earth;[7] [for thy heritage is (to be) over those existing with thee being born with the stars and clouds,[8] with the men whose

---

[1] Cf. John viii. 44 ("he [the Devil] is a liar and the father thereof"). Satan—here Azazel—is *par excellence* "the slanderer" (ὁ διάβολος), "he who slandereth truth."

[2] The fallen angels (1 Enoch vii., lxix. 6 ff.), and especially Azazel (1 Enoch viii. 1), are represented as having brought moral ruin upon the earth by teaching men the use of magic, astrology, and science (including the use of warlike weapons). A close parallel to our text exists in 1 Enoch ix. 6: "See what Azazel hath done, how he hath taught all unrighteousness on earth and revealed the secret things of the world which were wrought in the heavens."

[3] So Sammael, "the great prince in heaven," is reproached by the Torah for rebellion against God (*Pirḳe de R. Eliezer* xiii.: "The Torah began to cry aloud saying: *Why, O Sammael! now that the world is created, is it the time to rebel against the Omnipresent? Is it like a time when thou shouldest lift up thyself on high* (Job xxxix. 18)?"). Thus the two chief sins of Azazel consist in "scattering the secrets of heaven upon the earth," and in devising rebellion against the Most High.

[4] = probably LXX. ὁ ἰσχυρός (Heb. $h\bar{a}$ '$\bar{e}l$); see chap. viii. note [1]. Kohler suggests Heb. *'abir*, "Mighty One" (of Jacob), Gen. xlix. 24 (LXX, ὁ δυνάστης), Is. xlix. 26 (LXX, ἰσχύς).

[5] Bracketed clause attested by A K, omitted by S.

[6] Azazel is condemned to be in himself the fire of Hell; cf. xxxi. ("burnt with the fire of Azazel's tongue"). Thus wherever he goes he, as it were, carries Hell with him—a conception that appears to be peculiar to our Apocalypse in early apocalyptic literature (cf. Volz, p. 291).

[7] *i.e.* into those parts of the earth reserved for him till the final judgement. In 1 Enoch x. 4 Azazel is condemned to be bound and placed in Dudâêl, in the desert, and there to be imprisoned in darkness till the final judgement.

[8] This expression is obscure. It apparently refers to the men who belong (? by birth) to Azazel, whose lot has been pre-determined (see next note).

portion thou art, and (who) through thy being exist;[1] and thine enmity is justification. On this account by thy perdition disappear from me." And I uttered the words which the angel had taught me. And he said: "Abraham!" And I said: "Here am I, thy servant."][2]

And the angel said to me: "Answer him not; for God hath given him power (lit. will) over those who do answer him."[3] [And the angel spake to me a second time and said: "Now rather, however much he speak to thee, answer him not, that his will may have no free course in thee, because the Eternal and Mighty One hath given him [4]weight and will;[4] answer him not." I did what was commanded me by the angel;][5] and however much he spake to me, I answered him [6]nothing whatsoever.[6]

Abraham and the Angel ascend on the Wings of the Birds to Heaven (Chapters XV.–XVI.).

XV. And it came to pass *when the sun went down, and lo! a smoke as of a furnace*.[7] And the angels who had the portions of the sacrifice [8] ascended from the top of the smoking furnace. And the Angel took

---

[1] The wicked are Azazel's "portion," *i.e.* they have been assigned to him from the beginning. The idea seems to be predestinarian; cf. *Wisdom* ii. 24 ("by the envy of the devil death entered into the world, and *they that are his portion* make trial thereof"), *Ap. Bar.* xlii. 7 ("for corruption will take those that belong to it, and life those that belong to it"); 1 Enoch xli. 8. [Does the phrase in the previous clause, "being born with the stars and clouds," mean those who by birth and creation belong to the sphere of night and darkness, as opposed to the righteous, who belong to the realm of light? See 1 Enoch xli. 8 and Charles's note.]

[2] The bracketed clause is attested by A K, but is absent from S. It may be a later interpolation (but see Introduction).

[3] A fine psychological touch.

[4-4] The text may be corrupt. It might mean an overpowering will.

[5] The bracketed clause is attested by A K, but is absent from S. It is obviously a parallel and alternative text to the preceding clause.

[6 6] According to Sreznevsky's reading (*no se ni ti*, lit. "not this nor that").

[7] Cf. Gen. xv. 17 (also xv. 12).   [8] Cf. chap. xii. above.

me with the [1] right hand and set me on the right wing of the pigeon, and set himself on the left [2] wing of the turtle dove, which (birds) had neither been slaughtered nor divided. And he bore me to the borders of the flaming fire [and we ascended as with many winds to the heaven which was fixed upon the surface.[3] And I saw on the air] [4] on the height, to which we ascended a strong light, which it was impossible to describe,[5] and lo! in this light a fiercely burning fire for people, many people of male appearance,[6] all (constantly) changing in aspect and form, running and being transformed, and worshipping and crying with a sound of words which I knew not.[7]

XVI. And I said to the Angel: "Why [8] hast thou brought me up here now, because I [9] cannot now see, for I am already grown weak, and my spirit departeth from me?"[10] And he said to me: "Remain by me; fear not! And He whom thou seest come straight towards us with great voice of holiness [11]—that is the

---

[1] A, *his*.   [2] A omits.

[3] *i.e.* ? the heaven above the firmament.

[4] Omitted accidentally in S by homoioteleuton ("ascended . . . ascended").

[5] *i.e.* the uncreated light, which originally illuminated the earth, but was withdrawn when Adam sinned. See further notes on xvii. below.   [6] K, *sex*.

[7] The description refers to the host of angels who are born daily, sing their song of praise before God, and then disappear; cf. *Genesis rabba* lxxviii. 1: *Rabbi Helbo in the name of R. Samuel bar Nahman said:* "*One angel-host never repeats the song of praise, but every morning God creates a new angel-host and these cantillate a new song before Him and then disappear.*" They are created daily out of the stream of fire that proceeds from the holy *hayyoth* (*ibid.*); cf. Ps. civ. 4. Cf. also 2 Enoch xxix. 3: "And from the fire I made the ranks of the spiritual hosts, ten thousand angels, and their weapons are fiery, and their garment is a burning flame"; see further Weber, p. 166 f.

[8] S, *where*.   [9] K, *mine eyes*.

[10] The mortal man, conscious of his weakness, is blinded by the heavenly light. On the other hand, Adam, before he fell, was able to see by its aid "from one end of the world to the other" (T.B. *Hag.* 12a).

[11] *i.e.* proclaiming His holiness, so A; in S the word is corrupt. K (which may preserve the right reading here)

Eternal One who loveth thee; but Himself thou canst not see.[1] But let not thy spirit grow faint [on account of the loud crying],[2] for I am with thee, strengthening thee."

Abraham, taught by the Angel, utters the Celestial Song and prays for Enlightenment (Chapter XVII.).

XVII. And while he yet spake (and) lo ! fire [3] came against us [4] round about,[4] and a voice was in the fire *like a voice of many waters*,[5] like the sound of the sea in its uproar.[6] And the angel bent his head with me and worshipped.[7] And I desired to fall down upon the earth, and the high place, on which we stood, [at one moment rose upright,] [8] but at another rolled downwards.[9]

---

has: "[with a great voice] saying: *Holy, holy, holy is the Lord.*" In 1 Enoch xxxix. 12 the trisagion (Is. vi. 5) is the song of the angelic watchers.

[1] God is Himself invisible.   [2] Omitted by S.

[3] The Divine Presence is revealed by fire (Ex. iii. 2, Deut. iv. 36, Ps. lxxviii. 14), and God Himself is spoken of as " a consuming fire " (Deut. iv. 24, ix. 3). But here the fiery chariot which bore the Divine Presence is probably thought of; cf. Ezek. i. 4 (" a great cloud with a fire infolding itself ").

[4][4] A omits.

[5] Cf. Rev. i. 15 (Dan. x. 6). This feature is part of the supernatural colouring so characteristic of Apocalyptic—the heavenly light is of dazzling brilliance, the divine voice is like thunder (cf. 2 Enoch xxxix. 7: " like great thunder with continual agitation of the clouds "); see Volz, *Der Geist Gottes*, p. 120 f.   [6] Cf. Is. xvii. 12.

[7] A strongly Jewish touch—divine honour may be paid to God alone, and to none other, even the most exalted of heavenly beings; cf. Rev. xxii. 9.   [8] S omits.

[9] This description is interesting. The seer has ascended " as with many winds " to heaven, and is standing " on the height " (chap. xv.). He experiences a strong feeling of desire to fall down upon the earth, because the high place on which he is standing with the angel, at one moment rose upright, at another plunged downward (cf. 4 Ezra vi. 29 and 13–16). The commotion is produced by the Divine Voice. In chap. xxx. the seer finds himself suddenly (while God is speaking) again upon the earth.

And he said: "Only worship, Abraham, and utter the song which I have taught thee;" because there was no ¹ earth to fall upon. And I worshipped only, and uttered the song which he had taught me.² And he said: "Recite without ceasing." And I recited, and he ³ also himself ³ ⁴ with me ⁴ recited the song : ⁵

Eternal, mighty, Holy, El,⁶
⁷ God only—Supreme!
Thou who art self-originated,⁷ incorruptible, spotless,
Uncreate, immaculate, immortal,
Self-complete, self-illuminating;
⁸ Without father, without mother, unbegotten,⁸
Exalted, fiery One!

¹ A omits *no*.
² Only the angels understand how to utter the divine song of praise, though the blessed among mortals may (as here) be taught to sing thus in a state of ecstasy. Each of the angelic spheres has its own " Voice " (cf. 1 Enoch xl. 3 ff.), and the angelic language is incomprehensible to mortals (cf. chap. xv. above, end), though the illuminated and inspired seer may be taught both to understand and utter such " words " (as here; cf. ἐν γλώσσαις λαλεῖν in N.T.). The exalted Enoch in heaven underwent a similar experience (cf. 1 Enoch lxxi. 11 f. : " I fell on my face and my whole body melted away, but my spirit was transfigured, and I cried with a loud voice," etc.), as also did Isaiah (*Asc. Is.* viii. 17). According to Philo no beings can adequately express the praise due to God (*Life of Moses*, ii. xxxi. [§ 239]), contrast Ecclus. xxxix. 6. See further Volz, *op. cit.*, p. 137.
³ ³ A omits.
⁴ ⁴ S omits. In *Asc. Is.* viii. 17 the inspired seer joins with the angel in the celestial song of praise.
⁵ K, + *the first song of Abraham which I, the holy angel Jaoel, taught him (while) moving with him in the air.*
⁶ A K omit *El*.
⁷⁻⁷ Cf. the opening lines of the Jewish mediæval hymn, '*Adon 'ôlām*, " Lord of the world He reigned alone, while yet creation was unformed," and for " self-originated " the phrase " beginningless " (*bĕlî rē'shîth*) applied to God in the same context. The divine name *Shaddai* was traditionally explained as = " the self-sufficient " (*shĕ-dai hû lô*). This idea may underlie the text here.
⁸ ⁸ Cf. Heb. vii. 3, ἀπάτωρ ἀμήτωρ ἀγενεαλόγητος, of Melchizedek (= Heb. *bĕ'ēn 'āb bĕ'ēn 'ēm be'ēn yaḥas*). As Westcott remarks (*ad loc.*), " The words (ἀπάτωρ, ἀμήτωρ) were used

Lover of men,[1] benevolent,[2] bountiful,[3]
jealous over me and very compassionate;[4]
Eli, that is, My God—
Eternal, mighty holy Sabaoth,[5]
very glorious El, El, El, El, Jaoel![6]
Thou art He whom my soul hath loved!
Eternal Protector, shining like fire,
Whose voice is like the thunder,[7]

---

constantly in Greek mythology (*e. g.* of Athene and Hephæstus); and so passed into the loftier conceptions of the Deity, as in that of Trismegistus quoted by Lactantius (iv. 13): *ipse enim pater Deus et origo et principium rerum quoniam parentibus caret ἀπάτωρ atque ἀμήτωρ a Trismegisto verissime nominatur, quod ex nullo sit procreatus.*"

[1] = φιλάνθρωπον: cf. Wisdom i. 6 ("For Wisdom is a spirit that loveth men" [φιλάνθρωπον πνεῦμα]).

[2] = ? χρησπός.   [3] = χαριστικός.

[4] Cf. Deut. v. 9 f. The whole clause (from "lover of men" to "compassionate") contains a short summary of the divine attributes based upon Ex. xxxiv. 6, 7, a passage much used in later literature (cf. *e. g. Wisdom* xv. 1), and especially in the Liturgy; cf. 4 Ezra vii. 132–viii. 3 and the writer's notes thereon. These attributes are predicable especially of the Tetragrammaton (*Jahveh*), which connotes more particularly the elements of mercy and compassion, while *'Elōhim* denotes multiplied power (the Almighty), and is associated with the idea of justice and fixed law; *'El* is part of *'Elōhim* and denotes simply power.

[5] The use of *Sabaoth* alone as a designation of God is unusual, but not unexampled; cf. *Ex. rabba* iii. 6 [in answer to Moses' question, *What is His name?* Ex. iii. 13]: "The Holy One, blessed be He, said: Dost thou seek to know my name? I am called according to my deeds. I am called at various times by the names *'El Shaddai, Sabaoth, Elohim, Jahveh*. When I judge the creatures I am named *Elohim*, and when I wage war against the wicked I am called *Sabaoth*, and when I suspend (the punishment) of man's sins I am called *'El Shaddai*, and when I compassionate my world I am called *Jahveh*, because *Jahveh* means nought else but the attribute of compassion, as it is said (Ex. xxxiv. 6 f.) *Jahveh, Jahveh a God full of compassion*," etc.

[6] The fourfold *El* (attested only by S) looks like a substitution for the Tetragrammaton; *Jaoel* (here applied to God) is undoubtedly so. Elsewhere in this book it is the designation of the archangel.

[7] Cf. Note [3] at beginning of this chapter.

Whose look is like the lightning, all-seeing,[1]
Who receiveth the prayers of such as honour Thee!
[And turneth away from the requests of such as embarrass
with the embarrassment of their provocations,
Who dissolveth the confusions of the world [2] which arise
from the ungodly and righteous [3] in the corruptible age,[4]
renewing the age of the righteous! [5] [6]
Thou, O Light, shinest [7] before the light of the [8]
morning upon Thy creatures,

[1] Cf. Dan. x. 6 ("and his face as the appearance of lightning, and his eyes as lamps of fire") and Ezek. i. 13, 14.

[2] Lit. "the all" (Heb. *ha-kōl*); the expression is sometimes so used in the later Hebrew Liturgy.

[3] The mixture of good and evil, or rather of the righteous and ungodly, in this world, makes the present æon "corruptible" (cf. 4 Ezra iv. 26–30); even the righteous themselves suffer from contact with the godless—their holiness is dimmed.

[4] *i. e.* the present corruptible age (or "æon"); cf. 4 Ezra vii. 112, xiv. 13 ("the life that is corruptible").

[5] The confusions of the present world will be overcome by the elimination of the godless; then the renovated world (*i. e.* the present world purified) will become the fit habitation of the righteous. This view harmonises with the Rabbinical, which contemplated a renovation of the present world; see further Volz, *Eschatologie*, p. 297, and cf. *Jubilees, passim*.

[6] The bracketed clause is attested by A K, but omitted by S; it is probably an interpolation. The rhythm is much improved by its omission.

[7] Or "Thou shinest as Light"; the original Semitic text should probably be rendered "Thou didst shine." Light is the most striking feature in the highest heaven (cf. 2 Enoch xx. i, "I saw there a very great light," and xxxi. 2); God is Light (cf. 1 John i. 5). His majesty is surrounded with light to make Him invisible to all beings (*T. B. Megilla*, 19*b*). It is this heavenly light which is referred to here (cf. also *Wisdom* vii. 26 f., where Wisdom is represented as the radiance of the everlasting light). The first act of creation was when God "robed Himself with light as with a garment" (Ps. civ. 2), while the "radiance of His glory" (Heb. *ziv hădārô*) illumined the earth from one end to the other (cf. *Gen. rabba* iii., *Pirke de R. Eliezer* iii.). This heavenly light was afterwards withdrawn; the luminaries receive their light from a spark of it. For light as a symbol of blessedness cf. Volz, *Eschatologie*, p. 328. Ps. xix. contrasts natural (created) and spiritual light.

[8] Perhaps, as Ginzberg suggests, "before the morning light" is a mistranslation of the Semitic original "before

[so that it becometh [1] day upon the earth,] [2]
And in Thy [2] heavenly dwelling places there is no need of any other light
than (that) of the unspeakable splendour from the lights of Thy countenance.[3]
Accept my prayer [and be well-pleased with it],[4]
likewise also the sacrifice which Thou hast prepared Thee through me who sought Thee !
Accept me favourably, and shew me, and teach me,
And make known to Thy servant as thou hast promised me ! [5]

Abraham's Vision of the Divine Throne
(Chapter XVIII.).

XVIII. And [6] while I still recited the song, the mouth of the fire which was on the surface rose up on high. And I heard a voice like the roaring of the

---

the primæval morning " (*'ôr rîshôn* or *nĕhôrā ḳadmōniyyā*). The meaning of the original line would be that God at first illumined the earth with the heavenly radiance.

[1] Render *became*.
[2] S omits.
[3] Cf. Rev. xxii. 5, xxi. 23, Is. lx. 19 f. [The theme is expanded in the Synagogue Liturgy in connexion with the Benediction over light which precedes the recitation of the *Shema :* " Blessed art Thou, O Lord, who formest light and createst darkness. . . . Yea, eternal light (Heb. *'ôr 'ôlām*) in the treasury of life; for He spake, and out of darkness there was light."]
[4] The bracketed clause is attested by A K; S omits.
[5] Abraham prays that the sacrifice may be accepted, and as a result of this that the secrets of the future may be disclosed by revelation. The prayer seems to be a personal addition to the song of praise on the part of Abraham. The structure of the whole with its opening invocation, made up of clauses describing the divine attributes and transcendence, and followed by a prayer, is similar to that of 4 Ezra viii. 20 ff. (cf. especially verses 20–27), which is also poetical in form. Here it is to be noticed that the " song " proper appears to be a midrashic development of the divine attributes and character as deduced from the various names of God (*El Shaddai, Elohim, Jahveh, Sabaoth*).
[6] S omits.

62   APOCALYPSE OF ABRAHAM   [CHAP. XVIII

sea; nor did it cease on account of [1] the rich abundance [1] of the fire.[2] And as the fire raised itself up, ascending into the height, I saw under the fire a throne of fire,[3] and, round about it all-seeing ones,[4] reciting the song, and under the throne four fiery living creatures singing, and their appearance was one, *each one of them with four faces*.[5] And [6] such was the appearance of their countenances, *of a lion, of a man, of an ox, of an eagle :* [7] four heads [were upon their bodies] [8] [so that the four creatures had sixteen faces]; [9] and each had six wings; [10] from their shoulders, [and their sides] [11] and their loins. And with the (two) wings from their shoulders they covered their faces, and with the (two) wings which (sprang) from their loins they covered their feet, while the (two) middle wings they spread out for flying straightforward.[12] And when they had ended the singing, they looked at one another and threatened one another.[13] And it came to pass

[1.1] So A K; S is corrupt here.

[2] *i.e.* ? the voice was still audible even through the crackling of the fire.

[3] Cf. 2 Enoch xx. 3. The vision of God's throne of glory was the central point of the mystical experience.

[4] " The watchfulness of many eyes " (2 Enoch xx. 1), cf. Ezek. i. 18, x. 12 : the " Ophannim " (" Wheels ") are so described, and are regarded as an order of heavenly beings (like the Cherubim). But here the Cherubim are probably meant.

[5] Cf. Ezek. i. 5, 6.   [6] S K omit.
[7] Cf. Ezek. i. 10 (Rev. iv. 7).   [8] S omits.
[9] The bracketed clause is attested by A K; S omits. It looks like a scribal gloss.

[10] So Rev. iv. 8 (based on Is. vi. 2); in Ezek. i. 6 the four " living creatures " have each four wings. Here S reads *three* (*i. e.* ? three pairs of wings).

[11] S omits.

[12] Cf. Is. vi. 2, Ezek. i. 11, 12.

[13] The underlying idea of this strange representation seems to be that of emulation and rivalry (in service). This may be illustrated from the Midrash *Tanḥuma* on Gen. ii. 4 (ed. Buber, p. 10), where in a comment on the verse *Dominion and fear are with him, he maketh peace in his high places* (Job xxv. 2) it is said : " *Dominion, i. e.* Michael, *and fear, i. e.* Gabriel; *who maketh peace in his high places,* even the celestials (*hā-'elyōnim*) need peace. The constellations rise :

when the angel who was with me saw that they were
threatening each other, he left me and went running
to them and turned the countenance of each living
creature from the countenance immediately confronting him, in order that they might not see their
countenances threatening each other.¹ And he taught
them the song of peace which ² hath its origin [in
the Eternal One].²

And as I stood alone and looked, I saw behind the
living creatures a chariot with fiery wheels, each wheel
full of eyes round about; ³ and over the wheels was a
throne; ⁴ which I saw, and this was covered with
fire, and fire encircled it round about,⁵ and lo ! an
indescribable fire environed a fiery host. And I
heard its holy voice like the voice of a man.⁶

God discloses to Abraham the Powers of Heaven (Chapter XIX.).

XIX. And a voice came to me out of the midst of
the fire, saying : " Abraham, Abraham ! " I said :

Taurus says, " I am first, and I see what is before him ";
the *Gemini* say, " I am first, and I see what is before him ";
and so every single one says, " I am first " (corrected text). It
is to be noted that in the mystical Hebrew literature concerned
with the theme of the Divine Chariot and Throne (*Merkaba*)
the angels who guard the Chariot are represented as fierce
and warlike in aspect—flames dart forth from their eyes,
and they are armed with fiery weapons (cf. Jellinek, *Beth
ha-Midrash* iii. 94 f.). See further Additional Note II (p. 87).

¹ The relative position of the celestial beings about the
divine throne is thus described in the Liturgy : " The
hayyoth [' living creatures '] sing : the Cherubim glorify :
the Seraphim exult, and the Arelim bless. The face of
every *hayya*, Ophan, and Cherub is set toward the Seraphim,
and thus confronting each the other, they utter praise and say,
Blessed be the glory of the Lord from His place" (*Service of
the Synagogue, Festival Prayers* (New Year), p. 87 (ed. Davis)).

²-² Lit. *which is in itself* [*of the Eternal One*] : S omits the
bracketed words.

³ Cf. Ezek. i. 15, 18, x. 9, 12.
⁴ Cf. Ezek. i. 26.
⁵ Cf. Ezek. i. 27.
⁶ Cf. Ezek. i. 28 (end) combined with i. 26.

"Here am I!"[1] And He said: "Consider the expanses which are under the firmament on which thou art (now) placed,[2] and see how on no single expanse is there any other but He whom thou hast sought, or who hath loved thee."[3] And while He[4] was yet speaking (and) lo! the expanses opened, and beneath me[5] the heavens. And I saw upon the seventh firmament upon which I stood a fire widely extended, and light, and dew, and a multitude of angels, and a power of invisible glory over the living creatures which I saw; but no other being did I see there.[6]

And I looked from the mountain [7]in which I stood [7] [downwards][8] to the sixth firmament, and saw there a multitude of angels, of (pure) spirit, without bodies, who carried out the commands of the fiery angels who were upon the eighth [9]firmament, as I was standing suspended over them. And

[1] Cf. Ex. iii. 4, 4 Ezra xiv. 1 (K, + *Lord*).
[2] Abraham is now presumably " placed " in the seventh heaven, and surveys from above what is disclosed to him as existing in the various firmaments below him, and in the earth (the angels, celestial bodies, and everything that is moving on the earth).
[3] ? God is the sole controller of all these, and in this sense is the only reality.
[4] A K *this (voice)*.
[5] A, *them*.
[6] In *Asc. Is.* vii. 7 f. it is said that Isaiah saw in the seventh heaven " a wonderful light and angels innumerable," and " all the righteous from the time of Adam " (including Abel and Enoch); in *T. B. Ḥag.* 12*b* the seventh heaven ('*Araboth*) contains judgement and righteousness, the treasures of life, peace, and blessing, the souls of the departed righteous, the spirits and souls yet unborn, the dew with which God will awake the dead, the Seraphim, Ophannim, *Ḥayyoth*, and other angels of service, and God Himself sitting on the Throne of Glory. No doubt the " dew " in our passage is the resurrection-dew. Fire and light are much dwelt upon in this connexion. Possibly this mystical literature was influenced by the cult of Mithra, who was especially the God of Light.
[7.7] Lit. *of my standing*.
[8] S omits.
[9] *eighth* can hardly be right: read ? *seventh*.

behold, upon this firmament ¹ there were no other powers ¹ of (any) other form, but only angels of (pure) spirit, like the power which I saw on the seventh firmament.² And He commanded ³ that the sixth firmament ⁴ should be taken away.³ And I saw there, on the fifth firmament,⁴ the powers of the stars which carry out the commands laid upon them, and the elements of the earth obeyed them.⁵

The Promise of a Seed (Chapter XX.).

XX. And the Eternal Mighty One said to me: "Abraham, Abraham!" And I said: "Here am I." [And He said:] ⁶ "Consider from above *the stars* which are beneath thee, and *number*,⁷ them [for me],⁸ and make known [to me] ⁸ their number." And I said: "When can I? For I am but a man [of dust and ashes].⁹ And he said to me: "As the number of the stars and their power, (so will) I make thy seed a nation ¹⁰ and a people, set apart for me in my heritage with Azazel." ¹¹

¹⁻¹ So A; S, *their powers were not.*

² In 2 Enoch xix. the seer describes what he saw in the sixth heaven: legions of angels more resplendent than the sun, the archangels set over the sun, stars, seasons, rivers, vegetation, the living things and the souls of men, with six phœnixes, seven cherubim, and seven *ḥayyoth* in the midst, all singing with a voice indescribably beautiful; cf. also *Asc. Is.* viii. 1 ff, 6 ff., where the sixth heaven is described as full of hosts of angels uttering praise. In our passage apparently the angels of service (ministering angels) are located in this heaven.

³⁻³ A K, *the sixth firmament and it went away:* S reads *third* for *sixth*. ⁴ Lit. *surface.*

⁵ In *T. B. Ḥag.* 12b the sun, moon, and stars are located in the second heaven; in 2 Enoch xi. 1–5 "the course of the sun" and the angels "which wait upon the sun" are located in the fourth heaven.

⁶ S omits; K, + *to me.* ⁷ Cf. Gen. xv. 5. ⁸ S omits.

⁹ Cf. Gen. xviii. 27, 4 Ezra iv. 5, 6. The bracketed clause is attested by A K, but omitted by S.

¹⁰ Cf. Gen. xv. 5 (the MSS. read *for thy seed* instead of *thy seed*). S adds (after *nation*) *of people* wrongly.

¹¹ The underlying idea seems to be that God's heritage, the created world, is, under the conditions of sin, "shared"

And I said: "O Eternal, Mighty One! Let thy servant speak before Thee, and let not Thine anger kindle against Thy chosen one![1] Lo, before Thou leddest me up Azazel inveighed against me. How, then, while he is not now before Thee, hast Thou constituted Thyself with him?"

A Vision of Sin and Paradise: the Mirror of the World (Chapter XXI.).

XXI. And He said to me: "Look, now, beneath thy feet at the firmaments[2] and understand[3] the creation[4] foreshadowed[5] in this expanse, the creatures existing on it, and the age[6] prepared according to it." And I saw beneath [the surfaces of the[7] feet, and I saw beneath][8] the sixth heaven[9] and what was therein,[10] and then the earth and its fruits, and what moved upon it and its animate beings;[11] and the power of its men, and the ungodliness of their souls, and their righteous deeds [and the beginnings of their works],[12] and the lower regions[13] and the perdition therein, the Abyss[14] and its torments. I saw there the sea and its

---

with Azazel (see further Introduction, p. xxxii), *i.e.* it is largely under the dominion of evil powers. This is one of the fundamental conceptions of Apocalyptic. On the other hand, the Chosen People—who are ideally identified with the righteous—redeem the world, and in themselves make it once again fit to be God's heritage. From another point of view the same question is discussed in 4 Ezra—the problem, why, if the world was created for Israel, is Israel disinherited? (cf. 4 Ezra vi. 38–59).

[1] Cf. Gen. xviii. 32.   [2] Lit. *surface*.   [3] + *now*.
[4] Slavonic text, *creature*.   [5] Or *represented*.
[6] So S; A K, *ages* ("æon," "æons").
[7] K, *my*.   [8] S omits.
[9] A K, the *likeness of heaven* (or for *the sixth heaven* render *the six heavens*).
[10] A, *what was with it*.   [11] = ? "its spirits" (Bonwetsch).
[12] The bracketed clause is attested by A K; S omits.
[13] Cf. *Ephesians* iv. 9 ("the lower parts of the earth").
[14] *i.e.* Tartarus; cf. 2 Enoch xxviii. 3, xxix. 5. The "Abyss" is described in 1 Enoch xviii. 11–16 (xxi. 1–6, xc. 25, 26), where it is the abode of the impure angels; cf. Luke viii. 31; Rev. ix. 1, xi. 7.

islands, and its monsters and its fishes, and Leviathan and his dominion,[1] and his camping-ground, and his caves, and the world which lay upon him,[2] and his movements, and the destructions of the world on his account.[3] I saw there streams and the rising of their waters, and their windings. And I saw there the Garden of Eden and its fruits, the source [4] of the stream issuing from it, and its trees and their bloom, and those who behaved righteously. And I saw therein their foods and blessedness.[5] And I saw there a great multitude — men and women and children [half of them on the right side of the picture] [6] and half of them on the left side of the picture.[7]

[1] Or *possession*. Leviathan's dwelling is "in the lowest waters" (*Pirḳe de R. Eliezer* ix.). All the great sea-monsters in the sea are Leviathan's food, one being devoured every day (*ibid.*).

[2] "and between its [Leviathan's] fins rests the middle bar of the earth" (*op. cit., ibid.*).

[3] When Leviathan is hungry, one haggadic saying runs, "it sends forth from its mouth a heat so great as to make all the waters of the deep boil." [The two great monsters in the original form of the legend were Behemoth (the male) and Leviathan (the female): cf. Job xl.–xli.; 1 Enoch lx. 7 f.; *Ap. Bar.* xxix. 4. In the Rabbinical form of the Haggada (cf. *T. B. Baba bathra* 74*b*) each monster was multiplied into a pair, male and female; but they were rendered incapable of producing any progeny, lest by so doing they should "destroy the world." The female leviathan was killed and reserved for the righteous in the world to come; the male leviathan will not be slain till the last; see further 4 Ezra vi. 49–52, and the writer's discussion in *E.A.*, pp. 90 ff., with references. [4] A, *sources*.

[5] The heavenly Paradise is referred to which is to be the abode of the righteous ("those who behaved righteously"), whose fruits are "incorruptible" (4 Ezra vii. 123), wherein is "the tree of life" (Rev. ii. 7) whose "leaves are for the healing of the nations" (Rev. xxii. 2). In 2 Enoch viii. 2 the seer describes how he saw in Paradise "all the trees of beautiful colours and their fruits ripe and fragrant, and all kinds of food which they produced, springing up with delightful fragrance." Note that Paradise is here located on the earth, though the transcendental Paradise is meant; see *E.A.*, p. 196.

[6] The bracketed clause is omitted (accidentally) in S.

[7] The whole world is divided into two parts; the people of God on the right half, and the nations on the left.

The Fall of Man and its Sequel
(Chapters XXII.–XXV.).

XXII. And I said: "O Eternal, Mighty One! What is this picture of the creatures?" And He said to me: "This is my will with regard to those who exist in the (divine) world-counsel,[1] and it seemed well-pleasing before my sight, and then afterwards I gave commandment to them through my Word.[2] And it came to pass whatever I had determined to be, was already planned beforehand in this (picture), and it stood before me ere it was created, as thou hast seen."[3]

And I said: "O Lord, mighty and eternal! Who are the people in this picture on this side and on

---

The latter (= the heathen) are Azazel's portion (cf. chap. xxxi.).

[1] Emended text (Bonwetsch); MSS. read *in the light*.

[2] Note this hypostasising use of *Word* developed from such passages as Ps. xxxii. 6; cf. Heb. xi. 3, 2 Pet. iii. 5, 4 Ezra vi. 38.

[3] The whole conception is strongly predestinarian; the whole course of creation—the rise of evil, and the coming of the righteous—is predetermined; cf. 1 Enoch xciii., cvi. 19, cvii. 1, and Charles's note on 1 Enoch xlvii. 3. A strong expression of this idea occurs in 4 Ezra iv. 36, 37. For the "picture" of our passage we may perhaps compare the "pattern" (ὑπόδειγμα) of Heb. viii. 5 (Ex. xxv. 40, xxvi. 30, Acts vii. 44). In the Rabbinical literature Israel's election is spoken of as predestined before the creation of the world, and this idea is applied to certain other things, such as the name of the Messiah, the Torah, and repentance. In such connexions they often employ the figure of an architect and plans. One passage (*Gen. rabba* i.) runs: *When a man erects a building, at the time when the building is erected he enlarges it as it is erected, or otherwise he enlarges it below, and contracts it above: but the Holy One . . . does not act thus, but " the heavens " (which He created) were the heavens which had ascended in (His) thought, and " the earth " (which He created) was the earth which had ascended in His thought.* It was, however, the Essenes who insisted on an absolute predestination. The Rabbis, while allowing for a certain amount of predestination, emphasised man's moral freedom: "Everything is foreseen, but free will is given," as Akiba said.

that?" And He said to me: "These which are on the left side are the multitude of the peoples which have formerly been in existence and which are after thee destined,[1] some for judgement and restoration, and others for vengeance and destruction at the end of the world.[2] But these which are on the right side of the picture—they are the people set apart for me of the peoples with Azazel.[3] These are they whom I have ordained to be born of thee and to be called My People.

XXIII. "Now look again in the picture, who it is who seduced Eve and what is the fruit of the tree, [and][4] thou wilt know what there shall be, and how it shall be to thy seed [5] [6] among the people at the end of the days of the age,[6] and so far as thou canst not understand I will make known to thee, for thou art well-pleasing in my sight, and I will tell thee what is kept in my heart."

And I looked into the picture, and mine eyes ran to the side of the Garden of Eden. And I saw there a man very great in height and fearful in breadth, incomparable in aspect,[7] embracing a woman, who

[1] Lit. *prepared*.

[2] Of the peoples on the left side, who represent the heathen world as opposed to the Jews, some are to be spared at the final judgement, while the rest will be annihilated; cf. *Ap. Bar.* lxxii, 2, where it is said of the Messiah that *he will summon all the nations, and some of them He will spare, and some of them He will slay*. Sometimes (as in 4 Ezra xiii. 37 ff.) the whole heathen world is doomed to annihilation, and this view is very prominent in later Judaism. The idea of our text accords with the older view based upon such passages as Ps. lxxii. 11, 17; Is. lxvi. 12, 19–21 (cf. *Psalms of Solomon*, xvii. 34). Notice that our passage says nothing about the Messiah in this connexion.

[3] Cf. chap. xx. note [11].   [4] S omits.

[5] So A K, reading *sĕmeni*; S has *to thy name* (reading *imeni*).

[6-6] So S; but A K omit.

[7] Adam's great stature is often referred to in Rabbinical literature: "it reached" (when he was first created) "from one end of the world to the other," but when he sinned it was diminished (*T. B. Ḥag.* 12a); his manly beauty is also referred to *T. B. Baba meṣi'a* 84a).

likewise approximated to the aspect and shape of the man. And they were [1] standing under a tree of (the Garden of) Eden, and the fruit of this tree [2] was like the appearance of a bunch of grapes of the vine,[3] and behind the tree was standing as it were a serpent in form, having hands and feet like a man's,[4] and wings on its shoulders, six [5] on the right side and six [5] on the left,[6] and they were holding the grapes of the tree [7]in their hands,[7] and both were eating it whom I had seen embracing.

And I said: " Who are these mutually embracing, or who is this who is between them, or what is the fruit which they are eating, O Mighty Eternal One? "

And He said: " This is [8]the human world,[8] this is Adam, and this is their desire upon the earth, this

---

[1] K, + *both*. [2] Cf. Gen. iii. 6.

[3] Cf. *T. B. Berakoth* 40a, where it is recorded that R. Meir declared that the tree of which Adam ate was a vine, because the one thing that brings woe upon mankind is wine; cf. Gen. ix. 21 (" And he drank of the wine and was drunken "). So also the Greek, *Ap. Bar.* iv. 8 (cf. *Sanh.* 70a, *Bereshith rabba* xix. 8). The usual opinion was that the tree was a fig-tree; according to another view (*Gen. rabba* xi. 8) the fruit was barley; another (Samuel ben Isaac) a date. With this last agrees the *varia lectio* of A K here (" palm-tree ").

[4] Cf. *Gen. rabba* xx. 8 : " *Upon thy belly shalt thou go :* At the moment when the Holy One . . . said to the serpent *upon thy belly shalt thou go* the ministering angels descended and cut off its hands and its feet, and its cry went from one end of the world to the other." This legend was well known in antiquity. According to Syncellus (i. 14) the serpent had originally four feet; cf. also Josephus i. 1, 4, who declares that the serpent was deprived of both language and feet. For the punishment of the serpent see *Pirḳe de R. Eliezer* xiv. (ed. Friedlander, p. 99 and notes).

[5] v.l. *three*.

[6] This description really applies to Sammael (or Azazel), who had twelve wings (*Pirḳe de R. Eliezer* xiii.), and who descended and, finding the serpent skilful to do evil, mounted and rode upon it. Before its punishment by God the serpent had the appearance of a camel, according to the same authority (*ibid.*).

[7 7] A K omit.

[8 8] Lit. " council of the world," so K; A S, " light of the world." Adam (whose body is compounded of the four primal elements) is the microcosm.

is Eve; but he who is between them representeth ungodliness, their beginning (on the way) to perdition, even Azazel."[1]

And I said: "O Eternal, Mighty One! Why hast Thou given to such power to destroy the generation of men in their works upon the earth?"

And He said to me: "They who will (to do) evil —and how much I hated (it) in those who do it!— over them I gave him power, and to be beloved of them."[2]

And I answered and said: "O Eternal, Mighty One! Wherefore hast Thou willed to effect that evil should be desired in the hearts of men, since Thou indeed art angered over that which was willed by Thee, at him who is doing what is unprofitable in thy counsel[3]?"

XXIV. And He said to me: "Being angered at the nations[4] on thy account, and on account of the people of thy family who are (to be) separated after thee, as thou seest in the picture the burden (of destiny) that (is laid) upon them[5]—and I will tell thee what shall be, and how much shall be, in the last days. Look now at everything in the picture."

And I looked and saw there what was before me in creation; I saw Adam, and Eve existing with him, and with them the cunning Adversary,[6] and Cain who

[1] Azazel plays the part elsewhere assigned to Sammael; he uses the serpent as his instrument (cf. *Pirķe de R. Eliezer* xiii.).

[2] In chap. xiii. (end) the wicked (as distinguished from the righteous) are spoken of as those who "follow" Azazel, and "love" what he wills. They are Azazel's "portion." A striking feature of our book is the way in which the souls and bodies of men are represented as possessed by either good or evil powers.

[3] A K, *world* (which may be right). The word in S rendered *counsel* is an unusual one in this meaning.

[4] A, *men*.

[5] This apparently is the answer to the question given at the end of the previous chapter. God allows men to desire evil (with its inevitable punishment later) because of the treatment meted out by the nations to the chosen seed (Abraham and his descendants).

[6] Cf. 2 Cor. xi. 3 ("the serpent beguiled Eve in his craftiness").

acted lawlessly through the Adversary,[1] and the slaughtered Abel, (and) the destruction brought and caused upon him through the lawless one.[2] I saw there also Impurity,[3] and those who lust after it, and its pollution, and their jealousy, and the fire of their corruption in the lowest parts of the earth. I saw there Theft, and those who hasten after it, and the arrangement [of their retribution, the judgement of the Great Assize].[4] I saw there [5] naked men, the foreheads against each other, and their disgrace, and their passion which (they had) against each other, and their retribution. I saw there Desire, and in her hand the head of every kind of lawlessness [and her scorn and her waste assigned to perdition].[6]

XXV. I saw there the likeness of the idol of jealousy,[7] having the likeness of woodwork such as my father was wont to make, and its statue [8] was of glittering bronze; and before it a man, and he worshipped it; and in front of him an altar, and upon it a boy slain in the presence of the idol.

But I said to Him: "What is this idol, or what is the altar, or [9] who are they that are sacrificed,[9] or who is the sacrificer? Or what is the Temple

---

[1] According to *Pirḳe de R. Eliezer* xxi. Cain was the offspring of Eve and Sammael.

[2] In *Ep. Barnabas* xv. 5 the Devil is called "the Lawless One" (ὁ ἄνομος): *when His Son shall come, and shall abolish the time of the Lawless One* (cf. also 2 Thess. ii. 8).

[3] Notice that here and below certain evil tendencies are personified (Impurity, Theft, Desire; the catalogue seems to have been influenced by the Decalogue, Commandments vii., viii., x.). In later Kabbalistic books such tendencies are personified as demons; cf. *e. g. The Testament of Solomon*, § 34 (*J.Q.R.*, xi. 24; 1899), where seven female demons appear before Solomon bearing such names as "Deception," "Strife," "Jealousy," "Power."

[4] The bracketed clause is missing in S.

[5] A, *also* (instead of *there*).

[6] Omitted by S. Perhaps the clause is an interpolation; in any case the text appears to be corrupt. The word here rendered *scorn* (*moltshanie*, lit. "silence") is sometimes used in this sense, expressing "contempt," "scorn"; see D'yachenko's *Church Slavonic Dictionary*, s.v.

[7] Cf. Ezek. viii. 3, 5. [8] Or *body*.

[9-9] K, *who is the sacrificed one*.

which I see that is beautiful in art, and its beauty (being like) the glory that lieth beneath Thy [1] throne?"

And He said: "Hear, Abraham. This which thou seest, the Temple and altar and beauty, is my idea of the priesthood of my glorious Name, in which dwelleth every single prayer of man, and the rise of kings and prophets, and whatever sacrifice I ordain to be offered to me among my people who are to come out of thy generation.[2] But the statue which thou sawest is mine anger [3] wherewith the people [4] anger me who are to proceed for me from thee. But the man whom thou sawest slaughtering—that is he who inciteth murderous sacrifices,[5] of (sic) which are a witness [6] to me of the final judgement, even at the beginning of creation."

Why Sin is permitted (Chapter XXVI.).

XXVI. And I said: "O Eternal, Mighty One! Wherefore hast Thou established [7] that it should be so, and then proclaim the knowledge thereof?"

And He said to me: "Hear, Abraham; understand what I say to thee, and answer me as [8] I question thee. Why did thy father Terah not listen to thy voice, and (why) did he not cease from the devilish idolatry until he perished [and] [9] his whole household with him?"

And I said: "O Eternal, [Mighty One]! [9] (It

[1] S, *my* (a scribal mistake?).

[2] The whole sacrificial system and the Levitical cultus are of divine origin, and embody the divine ideal. The " rise of kings and prophets " is apparently involved in it as a subordinate development from it. The tone of the passage is reminiscent rather of *Jubilees*. In apocalyptic literature such allusions to the cultus are rare.

[3] " The image of jealousy " is correctly explained here as meaning the image which provokes God's jealousy or anger. Idolatrous practices in Israel are referred to.

[4] K omits *the people*.

[5] *i. e.* sacrifices involving the slaughter of human beings, such as the offering (through fire) of children to Moloch.

[6] A, *witnesses*.   [7] Or *ordained*.   [8] Lit. *what*.
[9] S omits.

was) entirely because he did not choose to listen to me; but I, too, did not follow his works."

And He said [to me]:[1] "Hear, Abraham. As the counsel[2] of thy father is in him, and as thy counsel is in thee, so also is the counsel of my will in me ready for the coming days, before thou hast knowledge of these,[3] or (canst) see with thine eyes what is future in them. How those of thy seed will be, look in the picture."

A Vision of Judgement and Salvation
(Chapter XXVII.).

XXVII. And I looked and saw: lo! the picture swayed and [from it][4] emerged, on its left side,[5] a heathen people, and they pillaged those who were on the right side, men and women and children: [some they slaughtered,][4] others they retained with themselves.[6] Lo! I saw them run towards them through four entrances,[7] and they burnt the Temple with

---

[1] S omits.   [2] *i.e.* "will."

[3] God's will is free, but so also is man's. The argument is interesting. From the fact, proved by the two contrary instances of Terah and Abraham, that man's will is free, the writer justifies God's freedom to permit sin, hinting, however, that the future will still further justify the divine counsel. The vision that follows (chap. xxvii.) serves to illustrate this.

[4] Omitted by S.

[5] The use of "right" and "left" throughout these chapters is notable. The conception of the right side being the source of light and purity, while the left is the source of darkness and impurity, is Gnostic, and passed from the Gnostics into the Kabbalah; see further Introduction p. xix. f.

[6] Sc. in slavery.

[7] So A K; S (*schody*), *descents* (= ? "generations"). The four "entrances" or "descents" by which the heathen make inroads upon the chosen people apparently correspond to the four hundred years of slavery for Israel predicted by God to Abraham in the vision of Gen. xv. (cf. vs. 13). This was interpreted by our apocalyptist, in accordance with current tradition, to refer to Israel's captivity and subjection by the four oppressive world-powers of the Book of Daniel, understood to be Babylon, Media, Greece, and Rome (cf. chap. ix. above, note [6]): thus the Palestinian Targum to Gen. xv. 13 runs: *And behold, Abram saw four kingdoms*

fire, and the holy things that were therein they plundered.[1]

And I said: "O Eternal One! Lo! the people (that spring) from me, whom Thou hast accepted, the hordes of the heathen do plunder, and some they kill, while others they hold fast as aliens,[2] and the Temple they have burnt with fire, and the beautiful things therein they do rob [and destroy].[3] O Eternal, Mighty One! If this be so, wherefore hast Thou now [4] lacerated [5] my heart, and why should this be so?"

And He said to me: "Hear, Abraham. What [6] [7] thou hast seen [7] shall happen on account of thy seed who anger me by reason of the statue which thou sawest, and on account of the human slaughter in the picture, through zeal in the Temple; [8] and as thou sawest [9] so shall it be." [9]

And I said: "O Eternal, Mighty One! May the works of evil (wrought) in ungodliness now pass by, but [10] (show me) [11] rather those who fulfilled the commandments, even the works of his (?) [12] righteousness. For thou canst do this."

---

which should arise to bring his sons into subjection. It is important to remember that the fourth "entrance" here corresponds to the Roman Empire [cf. also *Pirḳe de R. Eliezer* xxviii.]. Possibly "descent" (S) is the right reading here, and means "generation," a generation being roughly reckoned as equivalent to a hundred years: Heb. ? הוצאות.

[1] The writer obviously has in mind the operations of the Romans under Titus, which ended in the destruction of the Temple by fire in A.D. 70. For the burning and pillaging of the Temple cf. Josephus, *War*, vi. 4, 5 f.; cf. also 4 Ezra x. 21 f.

[2] Of those who were not killed in the Roman war, some were reserved for the victor's triumph, some for the arena, and the rest were sold as slaves; cf. Josephus, *War*, vi. 9, 2 f. [3] Omitted by S. [4] A, *from now onward*.

[5] K, *angered*. [6] Lit. *so much*. [7.7] A omits.

[8] Israel's captivity and sufferings are due to lapse into idolatry.

[9.9] So A K; but S omits. [10] A omits *but*.

[11] Something has fallen out of the text here.

[12] So A K; S, *this*. [The sentence *O Eternal Mighty One . . . his* (?) *righteousness* is rendered according to the text of A K; the text of S here is not in order.]

And He said to me: "The time of the righteous meeteth [them][1] first through[2] the holiness (flowing) from kings[3] and righteous-dealing rulers whom I at first created in order from such to rule among them.[3] But from these issue men who care for their interests,[4] as I have made known to thee and thou hast seen."

How long? (Chapters XXVIII.-XXIX.).

XXVIII. And I answered and said: "O Mighty, [Eternal One],[5] hallowed by Thy power! Be favourable to my petition, [for for this hast Thou brought me up here—and show me].[6] As Thou hast brought me up to Thy height, so make [this][5] known to me, Thy beloved one, as much as I ask—whether what I saw shall happen to them for long?"[7]

And He showed me a multitude of His people, and said to me: "On their account through four issues,[8] as thou sawest, I shall be provoked by them, and in these[9] my retribution for their deeds shall be (accomplished). But in the fourth outgoing[10] of a hundred years[11] and one hour of the age—the same is a hundred years[12]—it shall be in misfortune among

---

[1] So K; A, *him*; S omits.
[2] So S; A K, *the type (set) by*.
[3] The "kings" and "righteous-dealing rulers" referred to are, presumably, such as David, Hezekiah, and Josiah, under whose rule the claims of righteousness were recognised and the sovereignty of God, to some extent, realised.
[4] Lit. "for them" (= ? "for themselves")—from the righteous rulers spring sons who are faithless to their heritage (such as Manasseh). The sentence is obscure, and the meaning uncertain.
[5] S omits.
[6] Omitted accidentally in S (by homoioteleuton, "brought up . . . brought up").
[7] Cf. 4 Ezra iv. 33 ff.
[8] S K (*schody*) = *descents* (cf. chap. xxvii. note [7] above); cf. Gen. xv. 13-16: "four descents" = "four generations."
[9] Sc. four generations. [10] S, *descent* (as above).
[11] *i.e.* in the fourth generation (cf. Gen. xv. 16).
[12] In chap. xxx. the coming of the ten plagues on the heathen world is placed "at the passing over of the twelfth hour"; then follows (chap. xxxi.) the Messianic salvation. Apparently the present age is reckoned as enduring for

CHAP. XXVIII] PART II 77

the heathen [but one hour in mercy and contumely, as among the heathen]."¹

XXIX. And I said: "O Eternal [Mighty One]!² And how long a time is an hour of the Age?"³

And He said: "Twelve years⁴ have I ordained of this ungodly Age⁵ to rule among the heathen and

---

twelve hours (each hour = 100 years), *i.e.* one day (cf. John xi. 9). The apocalyptic writer may possibly reckon this day as beginning with the founding of the Holy City by David (cf. 4 Ezra x. 46) and culminating in the destruction of the last Temple by Titus, which calamity was to be followed by the period of woes described in chap. xxx., these bringing the present age (or æon) to a close. Now according to Josephus (*War*, vi. 10) the period from David's reign in Jerusalem to the destruction of the Temple by Titus amounted to 1179 years. If we suppose the seer to be writing at the close of the first or in the early years of the second century A.D. the period would include about 1200 years. Like all the apocalyptists he obviously supposes himself to be standing on the brink of the new age. Perhaps in the text above "and one hour of the Age" is intended to synchronise with the "fourth out-going of a hundred years." [In *Pirke de R. Eliezer* xxviii. a dictum ascribed to R. Elazar ben Azariah runs: (from Gen. xv.) thou mayest learn that the rule of these four kingdoms will only last one day, according to the Day of the Lord (= 1000 years).]

¹ The bracketed clause is attested by A K, but not by S. It may be an addition to the text. *Contumely* can hardly be right. Perhaps there was an error in the Greek text from which the Slavonic Version was made; ? τιμῇ misread ἀτιμίᾳ: read, then, "in mercy and honour."

² S omits.

³ This question has already been answered at the end of the previous chapter (one hour = 100 years); moreover, the reply that follows here does not really answer the question. There is probably something wrong in the text; "hours" and "years" seem to be confused. Perhaps the question originally ran somewhat as follows: *How much time is there (in) the hours of the age?*

⁴ ? Read *hours* for *years*. We may compare 4 Ezra xiv. 11 ("For the world-age is divided into twelve parts"), and the cloud and water vision in *Ap. Bar.* liii. f., where a similar division appears. If "years" be kept, each year will probably stand for a generation (reckoned at 100 years?); cf. 4 Ezra x. 45 (3000 years = 30 generations).

⁵ The present age is the age of ungodliness, where the organised forces of evil are dominant; cf. 1 Enoch xlviii. 7 ("the world of unrighteousness"), 4 Ezra iv. 29 f.

in thy seed; and until the end of the times it shall be as thou sawest. [1] *And do thou reckon and understand and look into the picture."*

And I [looked and] [2] *saw a man going out from the left side of the heathen;* [3] *and there went out men and women and children, from the side of the heathen, many hosts, and worshipped him.* [4] *And while I still looked there came out from the right side* [5] *(many), and some insulted that man, while some struck him* [6] *; others, however, worshipped him.* [And] [2] *I saw how these worshipped him, and Azazel ran and worshipped him, and having kissed his face he turned and stood behind him.* [7]

And I said: " O Eternal, Mighty One! Who is the man insulted and beaten, who is worshipped by the heathen with Azazel?"

[1] The passage printed in italic type that follows can only be regarded as a Christian interpolation (probably a Jewish-Christian one). [2] S omits.

[3] The man is clearly intended to be Jesus. His emerging " from the left side of the heathen " is curious. If the text is in order it must apparently refer to the emergence into prominence of the Early Christian Church in the Gentile world. It clearly cannot refer to racial origin, for it is stated further on in the chapter that " the man " sprang from Abraham's " generation " and God's people. But in view of the definite statement below—*this man from thy generation whom thou sawest (issue) from my people*—it is better to suppose that the text here is out of order: read ? *from the right side* and omit *of the heathen* as an incorrect gloss.

[4] *i. e.* His followers are to include large numbers from the Gentile world.

[5] *i. e.* from the Jewish world.   [6] Cf. Is. liii. 3.

[7] The worship of Christ by the Devil (Azazel) is a striking feature in this representation. It is difficult to determine its exact significance here. Does it reflect the Jewish-Christian feeling that the access of so large a part of the heathen world to Christianity endangered the purity of the new faith by inevitably bringing in its train a large admixture of heathenism ? It can hardly mean that Azazel had been truly converted. Indeed, his homage is significantly depicted as lip-homage (" kissed his face "; cf. the treacherous kiss of Judas). Perhaps the real meaning is that the kingdom of evil, and the Satanic powers, have been vanquished by Christ (cf. Luke x. 18, Phil. ii. 9, 10, Col. ii. 15, Ephes. i. 21 f.). The homage of Azazel—the head of the unredeemed heathen world—marked the triumph of Christ.

And He answered and said: "*Hear, Abraham! The man whom thou sawest insulted and beaten and again worshipped—that is the relief* [1] (*granted*) *by the heathen to the people who proceed from thee, in the last days,* [2] *in this twelfth hour* [3] *of the Age of ungodliness. But in the twelfth year* [3] *of my final Age* [4] *I will set up this man from thy generation, whom thou sawest* (*issue*) *from my people; this one all will follow,* [5] *and such as are called by me* [6] (*will*) *join,* (*even*) *those who change in their counsels.* [7] *And those whom thou sawest emerge from the left side of the picture—the meaning is:* [8] *There shall be many from the heathen who set their hopes upon him;* [9] *and as for those whom thou sawest from thy seed on the right side, some insulting and striking, others worshipping him—many of them shall be offended at him.* [10] *He, however, is testing* [11]

[1] = ἄνεσις (= Heb. *měnuḥā*).

[2] What is meant by *the relief* (*granted*) *by the heathen to the people who proceed from thee, in the last days?* The expression is difficult and obscure. Perhaps the "relief" spoken of means the mitigation of the process of "hardening" that has taken place in Israel (by its rejection of Jesus), which is brought about by the adhesion of some (a remnant) in Israel to the new faith, in conjunction with the great numbers who are streaming in from the Gentile world; cf. Rom. xi., especially xi. 25 ("a hardening in part hath befallen Israel until the fulness of the Gentiles be come in and all Israel shall be saved," and vss. 29-30: "For as ye in time past were disobedient . . . but now have obtained mercy by their disobedience, even so have these also now been disobedient that by the mercy shewn to you they also may obtain mercy").

[3-3] Omitted by A (homoioteleuton). For the confusion of "hour" and "year" see note [3] at the beginning of this chapter. [4] Lit. *of the Age of mine end.*

[5] Or "imitate," "become like."

[6] Cf. 2 Tim. i. 9 ("God who hath called us with a holy calling"), Ephes. iv. 1, 4, and often.

[7] *those who change in their counsels,* i. e. repent (μετανοεῖν = "change one's mind or will").

[8] Lit. "that (is)."

[9] Cf. Is. xi. 10 ("unto him shall the nations seek"), Matt. xii. 21, Rom. xv. 12.

[10] Cf. Matt. xi. 6, John vi. 66, Rom. xi. 8, etc.

[11] Cf. Rev. iii. 10 ("the season of trial that is coming upon the whole habitable earth"). The time of "trial" or "testing" referred to is, no doubt, the period of the Messianic woes which precedes the advent of the new age.

those who have worshipped him of thy seed, in that twelfth hour of the End,[1] with a view to shortening the Age of ungodliness.[2]

"Before the Age of the righteous beginneth to grow,[3] my judgement shall come upon the lawless heathen through the people of thy seed [4] who have been separated for me. In those days I will bring upon all creatures of the earth ten plagues,[5] through misfortune and disease and sighing of the grief of their soul. Thus much will I bring upon the generations of men that be upon it on account of the provocation and the corruption of its creatures,[6] whereby they

---

[1] *i.e.* the time immediately preceding the End of the present Age.

[2] Cf. Matt. xxiv. 22, *Ep. Barnabas* iv. 3, *Ap. Bar.* xx. 2 ("Therefore have I now taken away Sion in order that I may the more speedily visit the world in its season"). In the latter passage the fall of Jerusalem is regarded as hastening the End. Impatient longing for the End is characteristic of the Apocalyptists; see *e. g.* 4 Ezra iv. 33 ff.

[3] The coming Age is the "Age of the righteous" (for the expression cf. also chap. xvii. of our Book); it has been "prepared" for them (4 Ezra viii. 52), and they will inherit it (4 Ezra vii. 17). For the metaphor of growth in this connexion cf. 4 Ezra iv. 29, 35; the community of the righteous has already been "sown" (1 Enoch lxii. 8; cf. also 1 Enoch x. 16, "the plant of righteousness will appear"), but its full growth will only become visible after the judgement.

[4] Judgement on the heathen will be executed by the agency of Israel itself; cf. 1 Enoch xc. 19. In the Midrash *rabba* on Ruth ii. 19 a saying ascribed to R. Eliezer b. Jacob runs : "Vengeance on the nations of the world is in the hands of the Israelites (Ezek. xxv. 14)."

[5] A saying handed down in the name of R. Eleazar b. Pedath runs : "Just as the Holy One . . . brought (plagues) upon Egypt He will bring (plagues) upon this (wicked) nation [*i. e.* Rome], as it is said [Is. xxiii. 5] : ' As at the report from Egypt so shall they be pained at the report of Ṣor '" (read *Ṣār* "adversary," which is to be understood as meaning "Rome") : see Midrash *Tanḥuma*, ed. Buber, ii. 30; Bacher, *Pal. Amoräer* ii. 87. For a description of the plagues see the next chapter.

[6] On account of the sins of men God's anger must be visited upon the earth in judgement; cf. *Jubilees* xxiii. 22, etc. The idea that a time of great calamity and suffering would immediately precede the Messianic Age is a standing feature in Apocalyptic; cf. *e. g.* Matt. xxiv. 8, Mark xiii. 8 ("the birth-pangs of the Messiah").

provoke me. And then shall righteous men of thy seed be left [1] in the number which is kept secret by me,[2] hastening [3] in [4] the glory of My Name to the place prepared beforehand for them, which thou sawest devastated in the picture; [5] and they shall live and be established through sacrifices and gifts of righteousness and truth [6] in the Age of the righteous, and shall rejoice in Me continually; [7] and

[1] *i.e.* shall survive the Messianic "woes." The term "survive," "be left" (οἱ περιλειπόμενοι, *Vulg. qui residui sumus*, 1 Thess. iv. 15), became a technical one in Apocalyptic in this connexion; cf. 4 Ezra vi. 25, ix. 7, xiii. 16–24, 26, 48.

[2] The number of the elect righteous is pre-determined. This idea recurs in more than one form in Apocalyptic. Here apparently what is meant is that the number of elect righteous who shall survive the Messianic woes has been fixed beforehand, and is a secret known only to God. These living righteous shall enjoy the blessedness of the new Age upon the renovated earth (in Jerusalem). Nothing is said about the resurrection of the righteous dead to share in this felicity. In chap. xxi. the latter enjoy a blessed existence in the heavenly Paradise. Our Book apparently knows nothing of a resurrection. On the other hand, in Rev. vi. 11 it is the number of the righteous *dead* (the martyrs) that is predetermined. Another application of the same idea is to the whole number of mankind who are to be born, which is predetermined; cf. *Ap. Bar.* xxiii. 4. For those who survive the period of calamity, and share in the bliss of the new Age, see 4 Ezra vi. 25, vii. 27, ix. 7 f., *Ap. Bar.* xxix. 2; but in none of these passages is their *number* said to have been fixed beforehand.

[3] Cf. 4 Ezra vii. 98.

[4] A K, *to.*

[5] By *the place prepared beforehand* (cf. Rev. xii. 6) is here meant Jerusalem (*which thou sawest devastated in the picture*), presumably the renovated city on a renovated earth. The expression *place prepared beforehand* certainly suggests the heavenly Jerusalem (cf. *Ap. Bar.* iv. 2–6), which according to Rev. xxi. 2, 9 f. is to descend from heaven upon the renovated earth. But this is not certain. Our Book may contemplate nothing more than the earthly Jerusalem transformed and glorified.

[6] The sacrificial cultus in a purified form will be revived in the new Jerusalem; cf. ? 1 Enoch xxv. 6 (" the fragrance thereof " = ? of the incense). Prayer for the restoration of the Temple and cultus is a central feature in the Jewish Liturgy.

[7] With the restoration of the cultus the righteous will enjoy the privilege of seeing God's glory continually.

they shall destroy those who have destroyed them,
And shall insult those who have insulted them,[1]

"And of those who defamed them they shall spit in the face, scorned by Me, while they (the righteous) shall behold Me full of joy, rejoicing with My people, and receiving those who return to Me [2] [in repentance].[3]

See, Abraham, what thou hast seen,
And [hear] [3] what thou hast heard,
And [take full knowledge of] [3] what thou hast come to know.
Go to thy heritage,[4]
And lo! I am with you for ever."

The Punishment of the Heathen and the Ingathering of Israel (Chapters XXX.–XXXI.).

XXX. But while He was still speaking, I found myself upon the earth. And I said: "O Eternal, [Mighty One],[5] I am no longer in the glory in which I was (while) on high, and what my soul longed to understand in mine heart I do not understand."

And He said to me: "What is desired in thine [6] heart I will tell thee, because thou hast sought to see the ten plagues which I have prepared for the heathen, and have prepared beforehand [7] at the passing over of the twelfth hour [8] of the earth. Hear what I divulge to thee, so shall it come to pass:[9] the

---

[1] Cf. *Jubilees* xxiii. 30 and see note [4] p. 80.
[2] ? Heathen who are converted. [3] S omits.
[4] Cf. Gen. xv. 15 (*Thou shalt go to thy father in peace*); A K, *my*.
[5] S omits. [6] A K, *mine*.
[7] These also have been pre-determined.
[8] *i.e.* the last hour of the present Age.
[9] It is God's property to announce beforehand what is to occur and then to bring it to pass; cf. Justin Martyr, *Apology* i. 14 (end): *For this . . . is the work of God to declare a thing shall come to be long before it is in being, and then to bring about that thing to pass according to the same declaration.* Cf. also 4 Ezra ix. 6 (Gunkel's rendering of the " times of the Most High "): *their beginning is in word* (*i. e.* the prophetic word) *and portents, but their end in deeds and marvels*.

first[1] (is) pain of great distress;[2] the second, conflagration of many cities;[3] the third, destruction and pestilence of animals[4]; the fourth, hunger of the whole world and of its people[5]; the fifth by destruction among its rulers,[6] destruction by earthquake[7] and the sword; the sixth, multiplication of hail and snow;[8] the seventh, the wild beasts will be their grave; the eighth, hunger and pestilence will alternate with their

[1] The ten " plagues " here enumerated mark the distressful period which precedes the advent of the new Age; they correspond to the " signs " which are a common feature in the traditional eschatology; cf. 4 Ezra iv. 52–v. 13, vi. 13–28, ix. 1–6, xiii. 16 ff., *Ap. Bar.* xxv.–xxvii., xlviii. 30–38, lxx., 1 Enoch xcix. 4 f., 7–10, c. 1–6 (Dan. xii.). The first of the Ezra passages just cited affords a good example of the contents of these descriptions. It depicts a time of commotions, and the general break-up of moral and religious forces; the heathen world-power (*i. e.* Rome) will be destroyed; there will be portents in nature, general chaos in society; monstrous and untimely births, the failure of the means of subsistence, and internecine strife; and wisdom and understanding will have perished from the earth. With our passage depicting ten plagues may be compared *T. B. Sanh.* 97*a*, which divides the period into seven years; in the first there will be rain on one city and no rain on another (cf. Amos iv. 7); in the second arrows of famine; in the third a great famine in which men, women, and children and pious will perish, and the Torah will be forgotten; in the fourth abundance and dearth; in the fifth great abundance, the people will eat and drink, and the Torah will return; in the sixth voices announcing the coming of the Messiah; in the seventh war, and at its end Messiah ben David will come. In the New Testament, besides the Apocalyptic passage in Matt. xxiv. 8–31 and parallels, there is a marked parallelism with the Apocalypse of the seven trumpets (Rev. viii. 6–ix. 21, x. 7, xi. 14–19), six of which mark partial judgements, while the seventh ushers in the final judgement. Several of the " trumpets " announce judgements like the Egyptian plagues.

[2] *i. e.* distressful pain, sickness.

[3] The fall of fire is one of the portents of the End in *Ap. Bar.* xxvii. 10; cf. the fiery hail of the seventh Egyptian plague (Ex. ix. 23 f.) and the " first trumpet " (Rev. viii. 6–7); cf. also Rev. xi. 19*b* (" great hail ").

[4] Cf. the fifth Egyptian plague (murrain among the cattle, Ex. ix. 1 ff.).

[5] Cf. 4 Ezra vi. 22, *Ap. Bar.* xxvii. 5–6, Matt. xxiv. 7.

[6] Cf. *Ap. Bar.* xxvii. 3, 4 Ezra ix. 3.

[7] Cf. *Ap. Bar.* xxvii. 7. [8] Cf. Ex. ix. 23 f.

84 APOCALYPSE OF ABRAHAM [CHAP. XXX

destruction; the ninth, punishment by the sword and flight[1] in distress; the tenth, [2]thunder and voices[2] and destructive earthquake.[3]

XXXI. "And then I will sound the trumpet[4] out of the air, and will send mine Elect One,[5] having in him all my power, one measure[6]; and this one shall summon[7] my despised people from the nations,[8] and I will burn with fire[9] those[10] who have insulted them and who have ruled among[11] them in (this) Age.

"And I will give those who have covered me with

---

[1] Cf. Matt. xxiv. 16.

[2-2] K, "voices of thunder."

[3] Cf. Rev. xi. 19b. [Perhaps the passage most closely parallel with our text is *Ap. Bar.* xxvii. 1–13.]

[4] The trumpet is blown to announce the Divine intervention and the coming of salvation; it is not a direct summons to the exiles to return (cf. Volz, p. 310); cf. Benediction X in the *Shĕmōnē 'Esrē* Prayer (Singer, p. 48): *Sound the great horn for our freedom; lift up the ensign to gather our exiles, and gather us from the four corners of the earth.*

[5] This title of the Messiah is a favourite one in the "Similitudes" of 1 Enoch; cf. 1 Enoch xlviii. 9, lv. 4, etc. It recurs as a Messianic title in Luke ix. 35, xxiii. 35, and goes back to Is. xlii. 1.

[6] *i. e.* a measure of all the divine attributes—he reflects in little the totality of the divine character. This is an exalted conception, but does not seem to imply more than that the Messiah is a divinely endowed man, full of the power of the Holy Spirit (Is. xi. 1), which makes him free from sin (*Ps. Sol.* xvii. 36 f.). He is not depicted as a supernatural angelic being like Metatron. He is sent by God at the appointed time; cf. *Ps. Sol.* xvii. 23, Gal. iv. 4, John xvii. 3.

[7] Note that it is the Messiah here who summons the outcast Israelites from the nations (so also *Ps. Sol.* xvii. 28, Matt. xxiv. 31, 4 Ezra xiii. 39). More usually this is performed by God Himself (cf. the prayer cited in note [4] above).

[8] Cf. Is. lx. 4.

[9] Punishment of the godless by fire at God's hands is a common feature in the eschatology. It is the fire of the divine anger that is thought of, and is based upon Mal. iv. 1 (iii. 19); cf. the "fiery stream" and "flaming breath" which the Messiah emits from his mouth to destroy his enemies in 4 Ezra xiii. 10 (interpreted figuratively in verses 36 f.). A adds *through him* (after *I will*), *i. e.* through the Messiah; K, *through them*.

[10] *i. e.* the heathen nations.

[11] *i. e.* "over." Cf. *Ap. Bar.* lxxii. 6 ("But all those who have ruled over you . . . shall be given to the sword").

mockery to the scorn of the coming Age;[1] and I have prepared them to be food[2] for the fire of Hades and for ceaseless flight to and fro through the air in the underworld beneath the earth[3] [the body filled with worms.[4] For on them shall they see the righteousness of the Creator—those, namely, who have chosen to do my will, and those who have openly kept my[5] commandments,[6] (and) they shall rejoice with joy over the downfall of the men who still remain, who have followed the idols and their murders.[7] For they shall putrefy in the body of the evil worm Azazel,[8] and be burnt with the fire of Azazel's tongue;[9] for I hoped that they would come to me,[10] and

---

[1] Those who have scorned shall be scorned; cf. *Wisdom* iv. 18, Dan. xii. 2, *Ps. Sol.* ii. 32 f. ("the coming Age" is the Age of the righteous). Possibly renegade Jews are referred to, and are the subject of the remaining part of this chapter.

[2] Cf. Mal. iv. 1 (iii. 19).

[3] Here two conceptions seem to be mixed; there is (1) the idea of "the fire of Hades" (or Hell), which is located beneath the earth (for "Hades" = Hell in this sense; cf. *Ps. Sol.* xv. 11); this fire consumes their bodies; (2) combined with this is the idea of wandering (flying) restlessly about (properly in the air or outer darkness); cf. 4 Ezra vii. 80. In *T. B. Shabb.* 152b the souls of the wicked are said to be given no place of rest till the judgement. Here (at the word *earth*) S ends. The rest of the text (printed in small type) is found both in A and K.

[4] In Judith xvi. 17 "fire and worms" await the heathen enemies of Israel; cf. Ecclus. vii. 17, 1 Enoch xlvi. 6 ("darkness will be their dwelling and worms their bed"), Is. lxvi. 24. Here renegade Jews are probably meant.

[5] A, *thy*.   [6] Cf. Is. lxvi. 24, 4 Ezra vii. 93.

[7] The renegade Jews here referred to are described as idolaters (cf. Ezek. xx. 16, Jer. vii. 9); and the righteous rejoice over their "downfall"; cf. 1 Enoch lvi. 8 ("Sheol will devour the sinners in the presence of the elect"), xciv. 10 ("Your creator will rejoice at your destruction"), xcvii. 2 ("the angels rejoice" over it), Is. lxvi. 24. Notice that idolatry and murder are here conjoined; cf. Acts xv. 29 (according to one view of the text).

[8] Cf. the Greek *Apocalypse of Baruch* iv. (the dragon of Hades, which devours the bodies of the ungodly). In 2 Enoch xlii. 1 the guardians of the gates of Hell are said to be "like great serpents."

[9] Here the Evil Spirit is identified with Hell; his tongue devours the ungodly; and he himself is "the burning coal of the furnace of the earth" (chap. xiv.). Hell (Gehenna) is essentially a place of fire; cf. Is. xxx. 33 and *Mekilta* to Ex. xiv. 21.   [10] ? in repentance.

not have loved and praised the strange (god),[1] and not have adhered to him for whom they were not allotted,[2] but (instead) they have forsaken the mighty Lord."

Conclusion (Chapter XXXII.)

XXXII. "Therefore hear, O Abraham, and see; lo! thy seventh generation [3] (shall) go with thee, and they shall go out into *a strange land, and they shall enslave them, and evil-intreat them* [4] as it were an hour of the Age of ungodliness [5] *but the nation whom they shall serve I will judge.*"] [6]

ADDITIONAL NOTES

I

I am he who hath been commanded to loosen Hades to destroy him who stareth at the dead.

This obscure clause, which occurs in Jaoel's speech in chap. x., is absent from S. The Slavonic text runs as follows—

*Az esmi povelĕvy razreshiti ada,
istliti divyaŝĉas mertvym.*

Dr. St. Clair Tisdall suggests the following rendering—

*I am commanded to loosen Hades,
to turn to corruption (by) gazing at the dead.*

Dr. Tisdall explains the meaning thus: "The speaker has power given to him to 'deliver over to corruption' the

---

[1] *i.e.* probably Azazel.

[2] This clearly indicates that renegade Jews are referred to. For a similar reference cf. 4 Ezra viii. 25-31. It would appear that large numbers of Jews had lapsed, after the fall of Jerusalem, into indifference, or even open apostasy; cf. the Rabbinical references to "the people of the land" (*'am hā-'āreṣ*).

[3] Including Abraham, the seven generations may be reckoned thus: Abraham, Isaac, Jacob, Levi, Kohath, Amram, Moses.

[4] Cf. Gen. xv. 13.

[5] *i.e.* ? 100 years; cf. chap. xxviii. end.

[6] Cf. Gen. xv. 14. K concludes with the following words: *And this, too, said the Lord: Hast thou heard, Abraham, what I have announced to thee, what shall befall thy people in the latter days? And Abraham heard the words of the Lord, and received them into his heart.*

bodies of the dead by gazing at them. The verb [rendered 'gazing'] strictly denotes *marvelling, admiring.*"

Mr. Landsman writes as follows: "The verb *diviyati* is used in Slavonic, meaning 'to be ferocious,' 'to rage'; *divyaščas* means thus 'to stare at' somebody in such a way that he is frightened by the ferocity of the look. It can be translated as Dr. Tisdall translates it, but does this rendering and interpretation harmonise with the context?" Mr. Landsman goes on to suggest that the second line refers to Death personified; cf. Ps. xlix. 14 (" Death shall be their shepherd ") and Rev. xx. 13, 14, where " Death and Hades " are " cast into the lake of fire." Then render—

I am he who hath been commanded to loosen Hades,
to destroy him [i. e. Death] who terrifieth the dead.

This yields an admirable sense, and is probably right. Jaoel thus claims to be commissioned to abolish the terrors of Hades and Death.

II

And when they [the Cherubim] *had ended the singing, they looked at one another and threatened one another. And it came to pass when the angel who was with me saw that they were threatening each other, he left me and went running to them, and turned the countenance of each living creature from the countenance immediately confronting him in order that they might not see their countenances threatening each other. And he taught them the song of peace which hath its origin in the Eternal One* (chap. xviii.).

In addition to the illustration given in note [13] (p. 62) on this passage, the following extract from *The Revelation of Moses (Gedulath Moshe),* translated by Dr. Gaster in *The Journal of the Royal Asiatic Society* for July 1893, p. 576 (" Hebrew Visions of Hell and Paradise ") may be quoted—

Moses went to the fifth heaven, and he saw there troops of angels, half of fire and half of snow; and the snow is above the fire without extinguishing it, for God maketh peace between them [as it is said: " He maketh peace in his high places," Job xxv. 2], *and all praise the Almighty.* Cf. also the Midrash *Debarim rabba* (to Deut. xx. 10), where with reference to the same passage of Job (xxv. 2) it is said : *Michael* [who presides over the water] *is altogether snow, Gabriel is altogether fire, and they stand next each other without being harmed on either side* (so also *Midrash rabba* to Cant. iii. 11); cf. also 2 Enoch xxix. 2.

APPENDIX I

THE LEGEND OF ABRAM'S CONVERSION FROM IDOLATRY

(Cf. Chapters I.–VIII. of our Book.)

ABRAM'S emergence from the prevalent idolatry early became the theme of legend, which has assumed various forms and was widespread. These are collected, with full references, in Beer's *Leben Abrahams* (Leipzig, 1859), Chaps. I. and II., and are well summarised in *J.E.* I. 84–87 (" Abraham in apocryphal and Rabbinical Literature ").

The earliest literary evidence appears to be some extracts from Jewish Alexandrine works cited by Josephus under the names of Hecataeus and Berosus, of the third and second centuries B.C., and summarised by him (*Ant.* I. 1, 7) : [*Abraham*] *was a person of great sagacity both for understanding all things and persuading his hearers, and not mistaken in his opinions ; for which reason he began to have higher notions of virtue than others had, and he determined to renew and to change the opinion all men happened then to have concerning God : for he was the first that ventured to publish this notion, that there was but one God, the Creator of the Universe ; and that as to other* [gods] *if they contributed anything to the happiness of men, that each of them afforded it only according to his appointment, and not by their own power. This his opinion was derived from the irregular phenomena that were visible both on land and sea, as well as those that happen to the sun, and moon, and all the heavenly bodies, thus :* " *If* [said he] *these bodies had power of their own, they would certainly take care of their own regular motions ; but since they do not preserve such regularity, they make it plain, that so far as they cooperate to our advantage, they do it not of their own abilities, but as they are subservient to him that commands them, to whom alone we ought justly to offer our honour and thanksgiving." For which doctrines, when the Chaldæans and other peoples of Mesopotamia raised a tumult against him, he thought fit to leave that country; and at the command, and by the assistance of God, he came and lived in the land of Canaan.*

Another early attestation of the legend occurs in *The Book of Jubilees*, probably dating from the close of the second century B. C. Here it is related (chap. xi. 16–xii) that Abraham as a child " began to understand the errors of the earth," and at the age of fourteen, in order not to be entangled in the idolatry, practised in connexion with astrology by the whole house of Nahor, separated from his father and family, and prayed to God to save him " from the errors of the children of men." He became an inventor of an improved method of sowing seed, by which it was preserved against the depredations of the ravens. He then made efforts to wean his father from idolatry, but Terah, though acknowledging that his son was right, was afraid to make a public renunciation, and told Abraham to keep silent. Being no more successful with his brothers, Abraham rose by night and set fire to the house of idols. His brother Haran in an attempt to save them perished in the fire, and was buried in Ur of the Chaldees.

Here we meet with a feature which provided a *motif* for various forms of the legend—viz. the fire which burnt the idols and their house. This is really derived from the etymological meaning of $Ur =$ " fire; " thus " Ur of the Chaldees " is taken to mean " fire of the Chaldees." In our Book the fire descends from heaven and burns the house and all in it (including Terah), Abraham alone escaping. In other forms of the legend Abraham is cast into the fire (by Nimrod), and is miraculously preserved. Philo's account of Abraham's conversion (*de Abrahamo*, § 15) is as follows : [1]

The Chaldæans were, above all nations, addicted to

[1] Yonge's translation, vol. ii. p. 417.

the study of astronomy, and attributed all events to the motions of the stars by which they fancied that all the things in the world were regulated, and accordingly they magnified the visible essence by the powers which numbers and the analogies of numbers contain, taking no account of the invisible essence appreciable only by the intellect. But while they were busied in investigating the arrangement existing in them with reference to the periodical revolutions of the sun and moon and the other planets and fixed-stars, and the changes of the seasons of the year, and the sympathy of the heavenly bodies with the things of earth, they were led to imagine that the world itself was God, in their impious philosophy comparing the creature to the Creator.

The man [Abraham] who had been bred up in this doctrine, and who for a long time had studied the philosophy of the Chaldæans, as if suddenly awaking from a deep slumber and opening the eye of the soul, and beginning to perceive a pure ray of light instead of profound darkness, followed the light, and saw what he had never seen before, a certain governor and director of the world standing above it (κατεῖδεν . . . τοῦ κόσμου τινὰ ἡνίοχον καὶ κυβερνήτην ἐφεστῶτα), *and guiding his own work in a salutary manner, and exerting his care and power in behalf of those parts of it which are worthy of divine superintendence.*

The legend is cited or referred to in many places in the Rabbinical Literature. The following extract from *Bereshith rabba* xxxviii. 19 (on Gen. xi. 28) is a good example:

And Haran died in the presence of his father Terah. R. Ḥiyya bar R. Idi of Joppa said: " Terah was a maker and seller of idols. On one occasion he went out somewhere, (and) set Abraham to sell in his place. A man came (and) wished to buy (an idol), and he (Abraham) said to him: ' How old art thou?' And he said: ' Fifty or sixty years.' [Abraham] said to him: ' Woe to the man who is sixty years old, and will worship (an image) a day old!' And (the buyer) was shamed and went his way. Another time there came a woman, carrying in her hand a dish of fine flour. ' Here thou art,' said she. ' Offer it (as an oblation) before them (*i. e.* before the gods).' [Abraham arose, took a club in his hand, and smashed all the images, and placed

APPENDIX

the club in the hand of the largest of them. When his father came back, he said to him: 'Who has done this to them?' He [Abraham] said to him: 'Why should I hide (the matter) from thee? A woman came carrying a dish of fine flour. And she said to me: "Here thou art: offer it (as an oblation) before them." I offered (it) before them. Then one said: "I will eat first," and another said: "I will eat first." The one who was greatest among them rose up, took a club, and smashed them.' And [Terah] said to him: 'Why wilt thou fool me? How should they understand (anything)?' [Abraham] said to him: 'Let not thy ears hear what thy mouth says!' [Terah] took him and delivered him to Nimrod. The latter said to him: 'We will worship the fire.' Abraham said to him: 'But we should (rather) worship water.' Nimrod said to him: 'We will worship the water.' [Abraham] said to him: 'If so, we ought to worship the cloud that bears the water.' Nimrod said to him: [' We will worship] the cloud.' He replied to him: 'If so, we ought to worship the wind; it scatters the cloud.' [Nimrod] said to him: [' We should worship] the wind.' He replied: 'We should worship man, who endures, (defies) the wind.' He replied: 'You are bandying words with me; I worship the fire only, (and) lo, I will cast thee into the midst of it; then, let the God whom thou worshippest come and deliver thee from it.' Haran was standing there in doubt. He said: 'At all events if Abraham is victorious I will say I am of Abraham's opinion; but if Nimrod is victorious I will say I am of Nimrod's opinion.' When Abraham descended into the fiery furnace and was delivered, they said to him: 'On whose side art thou?' He said to them: 'Abraham's.' They seized him and threw him into the fire. And his bowels were scorched, and it fell out that he died in the presence of his father. That is the meaning of the verse, *and Haran died in the presence of Terah his father*."

Another version of the same legend (cf. *Tanna debe Eliyaha* ii. 25, and see *J.E.* i. 86) runs as follows:

Terah was a manufacturer of idols and had them for sale. One day when Abraham was left in charge of the shop, an old man came to buy an idol. Abraham handed him one on the top, and he paid the price asked. "How old art thou?" Abraham asked. "Seventy years," he replied. "Thou fool," said Abraham; "how canst thou adore a god so much younger than thyself? Thou wert born seventy years ago, and this god was made yesterday." The buyer threw away the idol and received his money back. The other sons of Terah complained to their father that Abraham did not know how to sell the idols, and it was arranged that he should act as priest to the latter. One day a woman

APPENDIX

brought a meal-offering for the idols, and as they would not eat he exclaimed: *A mouth have they but speak not, eyes have they but see not, ears but hear not, hands but handle not. May their makers be like them, and all who trust in them* (Ps. cxv. 5–8); and he broke them in pieces, and burned them. Abraham was thereupon brought before Nimrod, who said: " Knowest thou not that I am god, and ruler of the world? Why hast thou destroyed my images? " Abraham replied: " If thou art god and ruler of the world, why dost thou not cause the sun to rise in the west and set in the east? If thou art god and ruler of the world, tell me all that I have now at heart, and what I shall do in the future? " Nimrod was dumbfounded, and Abraham continued: " Thou art the son of Cush, a mortal man. Thou couldst not save thy father from death, nor wilt thou thyself escape it."

Another form of the legend, after narrating the wonderful nature of Abraham's birth, Nimrod's alarm at the report of the astrologers and magicians in connexion therewith, and his attempt to bribe Terah to give up the child, who, under the charge of a nurse, was hidden by his father in a cave, where he remained for some years, proceeds (cf. *Midrash hagadol* on Genesis. ed. Schechter p. 189 f.):

When Abraham came forth from the cave, his mind was inquiring into the creation of the world, and he was intent upon all the luminaries of the world, to bow down to them and serve them, in order that he might know which of them was God. He saw the moon, whose light shone in the night from one end of the world to the other, and whose retinue [of shining stars] was so numerous. Said he: " This is God! " (and) he worshipped her all the night. But when at day-break he saw the sun-rise, and at its rising the moon become dark and her strength wane, he said: " The light of the moon only proceeds from the light of the sun, and the world is only sustained by the light of the sun," and so he worshipped the sun all day. At evening the sun set, and its power waned, and the moon and the stars and the constellations emerged (once more). Said [Abraham]: " Verily there is a Lord and a God over these."

A peculiar form of the legend occurs in the *Biblical Antiquities* of Pseudo-Philo vi. 5–18.[1]

According to this Midrashic account, Abram with eleven other men whose names are given, refused to bake bricks

---

[1] Edited for the first time in English by Dr. M. R. James, and published in this Series.

for the building of the Tower of Babel. In consequence, they were seized by the people of the land, and brought before the princes, and on their persistent refusal to take any part in the building of the Tower, were condemned to be burnt. A respite of seven days is given them at the intercession of Jectan, " the first prince of the captains," but at the end of this time, if they have not already changed their mind, they are to be handed over for execution. Jectan, a secret friend, contrives their escape to the mountains, and eleven of the men do escape, but Abram refuses to flee, and remains behind. At the end of the seven days, the " people of the land " demand that the imprisoned men shall be produced. Jectan explains that eleven of them " have broken prison and fled by night," but Abram is produced, is cast into the fire, but is miraculously delivered by God,[1] who causes an earthquake which breaks up the furnace and scatters the fire, which " consumed all them that stood round about in the sight of the furnace; and all they that were burned in that day were 83,500. But upon Abram was there not any the least hurt by the burning of the fire."

It is obvious from what has been adduced that the legend assumed different forms. The narrative just cited is quite independent of the rest, except for the episode of the fiery furnace. The form also given in our Book is largely independent. Nowhere else do we meet with the details about the idol-gods *Merumath* and *Barisat*. The fiery furnace also is absent, and the burning of the idols is effected by fire from heaven. At the same time in chap. vii. of our Book in the speech of Abraham to Terah about the claims to divinity of fire, water, earth, sun, moon, and stars, there is a marked parallelism with the Rabbinical accounts. It is clear that the form of the legend in our Book is due to an independent and free handling of the legendary material, many new features having been introduced in the process.

The legend also occurs in various forms in the Patristic and Mohammedan literature. For the former cf. *Clem. Recognitions*, i. 32 f., Augustine, *De Civitate* xvi. 15; and for the latter cf. *J.E.*, i. 87 f. (" Abraham in Mohammedan Legend "). See further Fabricius, *Codex pseudepigraphus*

---

[1] According to R. Eliezer b. Jacob it was Michael who delivered Abraham from the fire; but the prevailing view was that it was God Himself; cf. *Bereshith rabba* xliv. 16.

Vet. Test. (2nd ed., Hamburg, 1722, pp. 335-428), Bonwetsch, pp. 41-55. The later Jewish forms of the legend (as preserved in late Midrashim) have been collected and translated into German by Wünsche, *Aus Israels Lehrhallen* (1907), i. pp. 14-48 (the original Hebrew texts are printed mainly in Jellinek's *Beth ha-Midrash*); cf. also G. Friedlander, *Rabbinic Philosophy and Ethics* (1912), pp. 47 ff.

APPENDIX II [1]

All the Palæas begin the story of Abraham as follows:

"*But Terah begat Abraham:*" *and Terah began to do the same work which he saw (being done) in the case of his father Nahor, and worshipped the gods, and offered sacrifices before them, calves, and heifers, and performed everything well-pleasing to the Devil. When Abraham, however, had seen this, and on account of it fell into much reflexion, he said within himself: "These gods are wood, through which my father Terah is deceived, and these gods have no soul in themselves; and possessing eyes they see not, and having ears they hear not, and possessing hands they handle not, and having feet they go not, and possessing noses they smell not, and there is no voice in their mouth. Therefore I am of opinion that in truth my father Terah is deceived. But Abraham having thought thus. . . .*

Then some of the MSS. proceed:

Abraham (or I.), however, one day planed the gods, etc. (as in chap. i.); but the rest continue with chap. vii.: [*Having thought thus, Abraham*] *came to his father,* etc.

APPENDIX III [2]

A portion of our Apocalypse is contained in an abbreviated form in the Kukulevic MS. which is described by V. Jagic in his *Contributions to the History of the Literature of the Croat and Serbian People* (*Prilozi k historji knjizevnosti naroda hrvatskoga i srbskoga*), *Agram* 1868.

---

[1] See Bonwetsch, p. 9. [2] See Bonwetsch, pp. 9-11.

The MS. dates from the year 1520, and includes on pp. 37v foll. parts of *The Apocalypse of Abraham*, in a much abbreviated, dislocated and altered form as compared with the tradition represented by the Russian MSS. This apparently represents an independent South Slavonic Recension of our Book. It runs as follows : [1]

A word of righteous Abraham, as God loved Abraham. He was born ; in sixty years [i. e. *at the age of 60*] *He* [*God*] *had given him* (*Terah*) *a son,* (*even to Terah*) *who believed in the idols, and manufactured idols, and gave them names. Abraham went and sold the idols. When on a certain day Abraham had lain down in the field, and saw the stars of heaven and everything* (*made*) *by God, he surveyed it all in his heart, and said :* " *O great marvel ! These idols have not made it : heaven and earth and everything hath God made, we, however, are senseless men not believing in the Creator of heaven and earth, but we believe in stones and wood, and in vain things, but I see and understand that God is great, who hath created heaven and earth and the whole world."*

On a certain day his father carved idols, and told Abraham to prepare (*their*) *food. And Abraham took a god and stood him at the fire behind the pot, and said to him : If thou art a god, pay heed to the pot and to thyself. And then the pot boiled over, and burnt the god's head. And Abraham approached, and saw it, and laughed about it much, and said to his father :* " *Father, these idols are no good, they cannot protect themselves, how should they protect us ?"* *And his father was angry, and said :* " *Ills have befallen us, my son, I am not offended." And then Abraham arose and took the idols, and loaded them on an ass, and brought them into the street to sell. And he saw a great marsh, and said to the idols :* " *If you are gods, take heed to the ass that it do not drown you." And the ass went into the marsh and sank in the mire. And Abraham said to them :* " *If you were good gods,*

[1] As given in a German translation by Dr. L. Masing of Dorpat (in Bonwetsch, pp. 10 f.).

(*then*) *you would protect . . . and also protect yourselves; but since you are evil gods, you must suffer evil." And he took them and shattered them.*

And he returned to his father, and said: " Father, I tell thee the truth; these gods are no good, and you are wrong to believe in them." Thereupon his father flung a knife against him, and Abraham stood aside, and was perplexed in his mind. And he went into the land of Mesopotamia Chaldaea and did not know the way by which to go. Then the angel Uriel came to him, having made himself (*in appearance*) *like a traveller. And Abraham said to the angel: " Tell me, Brother, whence art thou, and whither goest thou?" The angel said to him: " I go to the land of Chaldaea." And Abraham said: " I also go with thee." And the angel said to him: " Come, Brother!" And Abraham saw a large* (*and*) *very black eagle sitting and nodding its head at Abraham; and Abraham passing by it was seized with great fear, and said nothing.*

And the angel said to him: " Talk, Brother, of nothing but God." And the angel taught him all the time to talk of nothing but godly things. And the angel said to him: " Yonder eagle was indeed the Devil himself, and desired to make thee turn back."

And in that land Abraham abode fifteen years; there he dwelt, (*and*) *thither his father came to him, and his brother Lot, and there Abraham took his wife Sarah.*

And the angel came to Abraham, and told him to depart from this land, and to go into the land of Chaldaea (sic), *" for there the Lord hath commanded thee to live."* Abraham did accordingly. The narrative then proceeds on the basis of the account given in Gen. xx.

It is obvious that this is largely an independent reshaping of the old material. But it contains clear reminiscences both of the legendary and apocalyptic parts of our Book.

INDEX

[The references are to pages, unless otherwise indicated; *n.* = " note " or " notes."]

ABBREVIATIONS, xxxii f.
Abraham—
  prominence of, in later Literature, xxiv
  legend of, ch. i–viii and Appendix I (cf. also p. 48 and notes)
  as maker of idols, 35 *n.*
  burns idol-temple, Appendix I (cf. p. 43)
  trance of (Gen. xv), 44 *n.*
  " Friend of God," 45 *n.*
Abraham, Apocalypse of—
  The Slavonic text, x ff.
  original language and date of, xv ff.
  early attestation of, xvi ff.
  Jewish and Essene character of, xxi
Abraham, Testament of—
  xix, xxiii, xxxi, 49 *n.*, 52 *n.*, 53 *n.*
Abyss, the, 66 *n.*
Adam, stature of, 69 *n.*
Age (the coming), " sown," 80 *n.*
Angelology, xxv f.
Angels = material altar, 51 *n.*
  worship of, 57 *n.*
Apostolic Constitutions cited, xviii
Asceticism in *Ap. Abr.*, xxix
Azazel, xxi, xxiii, xxvi, xxxii, 52 *n.*, 53 *n.*, 54 *n.*, 65 *n.*, 71 *n.*, 78 *n.*, 85

Barisat, xv, 39 f. and note, 41
Beliar, 52 *n.*

Cain, lawlessness of, xxiii, cf. 72 *n.*
Chariot, the divine, xxix f., 63 *n.*
Cherubim, 87. See also *Ḥayyoth*
Christ, worship of, 78 *n.*
Christological development, xxv, xxxi f.
Clementine Literature, xxxi

Day (= 1000 years), 77 *n.*
Dead, burial of the, 48 *n.*
Dew (the resurrection), 64 *n.*
" Descents " (= " generations "), 74 *n.*, 76 *n.*
Dove, the, 51 *n.*
Dualism, xxvi, 53 *n.*

Ebionites, xxi f.
Elect, number of the, predetermined, 81 *n.*
Enoch, falls into background, xxiv
  relation of, to Metatron, xxv
Essenes, xxiv, xxix, 68 *n.*

Fasting, 45 *n.*
Fire, theophanic, 57 *n.*
  as element of punishment, 84 *n.*
Food (heavenly), 50 *n.*

INDEX

Freedom, moral, 74 *n.*
Friend, see *Abraham*

Garments, heavenly, 53 *n.*
Ginzberg, cited, xxi f., *et al.*
Gnostic elements in *Ap. Abr.* xix f.
Gnostics, xvii ff., xxii f.

Hades, 86
Ḥayyoth ("living creatures"), 47 *n.*, 56 *n.*, 62 *n.*, 64 *n.*
Hell, 85 *n.*
Heathen, punishment of, xxviii, 69 *n.*, 80 *n.*
Heavens, the seven, 47 *n.*, 64 *n.*, 65 *n.*
"Hour" (= 100 years), 76 f. and note

Irenæus referred to, xix, xx

Jaoel (archangel) xxiii, xxv, 46 *n.* See also *Metatron*
James, Dr. M. R., quoted, xviii
Jealousy, image of, 73 *n.*
Jews, renegade, 85 *n.*, 86 *n.*
Judgement, the, xxvii f.

Kabbalah, xx, 72 *n.*
Kohler, quoted, xxiv, xxx

"Lawless One" (Devil), 72 *n.*
Leviathan, 48 *n.*, 67 *n.*
Light (created), 44 *n.*
  (uncreated), 56 *n.*, 60 *n.*, 64 *n.*
Light and darkness (opposition of), xix
Liturgy, Jewish, cited, 58 *n.*, 59 *n.*, 61 *n.*, 63 *n.*, 84 *n.*
Logos-idea, see *Christological development*

Merumath, xv, 35 *n.*, 41
Messiah—
  in line of Seth, xxiii
  gathers Israel, xxviii, (cf. ch. xxxi and notes)

Messian—
  endowed with a measure of the divine attributes, 84 *n.* (cf. also 69 *n.*)
Messianic Salvation, the, 76 *n.*, 84 *n.*
Metatron (Michael), xxv, 46 *n.*, 49 *n.* See further *Jaoel, Michael*
Michael, 47 *n.*, 48 *n.*, 49 *n.* See further *Metatron*
Midrash, cited, xxiv f., 35, 48 *n.*, 52 *n.*, 56 *n.*, 62 *n.*, 68 *n.*, 70 *n.*, 80 *n.*, 87
Mighty One (title of God), 43 *n.*, 54 *n.*, 55
Mishna cited, 38 *n.*
Mithra, cult of, 64 *n.*

Name, the divine, mystery of, xxiii
Names, the divine, mystical significance of, 55 f. and notes, 61 *n.*
Nicephorus, Stichometry of, xviii f., xxii

Ophannim ("Wheels"), 62 *n.*, 63 *n.*, 64 *n.*

Palaea, xii, 94
Paradise, the heavenly, xxvii, 67 *n.*
Philo cited, xvii, 50 *n.*, 58 *n.*
Plagues, the ten (at end of the Age), 76 *n.*, 80 *n.*, 83 *n.*
Porfir'ev, I., xiv
Predestinarian ideas in *Ap. Abr.*, 55 *n.*, 68 *n.*, 81 *n.*, 82 *n.*
Prediction, divine, 82 *n.*
Pypin, A., xiv

"Right and left," xx, 67 f. and note, 69 *n.*, 74 *n.*
Resurrection doctrine, absence of, in *Ap. Abr.*, xxvii, 81 *n.*

INDEX

Sabaoth, 59 *n.*
Sacrifices, human, 73 *n.*
Sacrificial system divine, 73 *n.* (cp. 81 *n.*)
Sammael, 54, 70 *n.*, 71 *n.*
Seth, line of, xxiii
Shaddai, 59 *n.*
Sin, original, xxvii, xxxi
Song (angelic), 46 *n.*, 56 *n.*, 58 *n.*, 87
Sreznevsky, J., xi
"Survive" (technical term in Apocalyptic), 81 *n.*
Sylvester, Codex, x, xi

Talmud, cited xxvii, 47 *n.*, 49 *n.*, 52 *n.*, 53 *n.*, 60 *n.*, 64 *n.*, 67 *n.*, 69 *n.*, 70 *n.*, 83 *n.*

Tartarus, see *Abyss*
Temple, burning of the, 75 *n.*
Throne (of God), vision of, ch. xviii, 62 *n.*, 64 *n.*
Tikhonravov, xi, xiv
Tree (of Paradise), = the vine, 70 *n.*
Trumpet, the, 84 *n.*

Ur (of the Chaldees), 43 *n.*

Wine and milk, 40 *n.*
"Woes" (Messianic), 81 *n.*
Word of God, 45 *n.*, 68 *n.*

Zohar, referred to, xx, 49 *n.*
Zoroastrianism, xix

TRANSLATIONS OF EARLY DOCUMENTS
SERIES I
PALESTINIAN JEWISH TEXTS
(PRE-RABBINIC)

THE ASCENSION OF ISAIAH

THE ASCENSION OF ISAIAH

BY

R. H. CHARLES, D.Litt., D.D.

CANON OF WESTMINSTER; FELLOW OF MERTON COLLEGE;
FELLOW OF THE BRITISH ACADEMY

WITH AN INTRODUCTION BY THE
Rev. G. H. BOX, M.A.

WIPF & STOCK · Eugene, Oregon

Wipf and Stock Publishers
199 W 8th Ave, Suite 3
Eugene, OR 97401

Apocalypse of Abraham
Together with The Ascension of Isaiah
By Box, G. H. and Landsman, J. I
Softcover ISBN-13: 978-1-6667-6658-5
Hardcover ISBN-13: 978-1-6667-6659-2
Publication date 12/2/2022
Previously published by SPCK, 1919

This edition is a scanned facsimile of
the original edition published in 1919.

EDITORS' PREFACE

THE object of this series of translations is primarily to furnish students with short, cheap, and and text-books, which, it is hoped, will facilitate t. study of the particular texts in class under co petent teachers. But it is also hoped that t volumes will be acceptable to the general reade who may be interested in the subjects with which they deal. It has been thought advisable, as a general rule, to restrict the notes and comments to a small compass; more especially as, in most cases, excellent works of a more elaborate character are available. Indeed, it is much to be desired that these translations may have the effect of inducing readers to study the larger works.

Our principal aim, in a word, is to make some difficult texts, important for the study of Christian origins, more generally accessible in faithful and scholarly translations.

In most cases these texts are not available in a cheap and handy form. In one or two cases texts have been included of books which are available in the official Apocrypha; but in every such case reasons exist for putting forth these texts in a new translation, with an Introduction, in this series.

We desire to express our thanks to Canon Charles and Messrs. A. & C. Black for their permission to reprint here the translation of the *Ascension of Isaiah*, published in 1900.

W. O. E. OESTERLEY.
G. H. BOX.

INTRODUCTION

Short Account of The Book

THE apocryphal book known as *The Ascension of Isaiah* appears to be a work of composite structure made up of three originally distinct parts, one of which is of Jewish, the others of Christian origin. The title given to the whole work—*The Ascension of Isaiah*—is due to the principal extant version, the Ethiopic. Strictly, however, it applies only to the last part, contained in chapters vi.–xi. ("The Vision of Isaiah"). The other two parts, which probably circulated independently at first, may be identified with writings (otherwise lost) known as *The Martyrdom of Isaiah* (= i. 1–iii. 12 and v. 1 *b*–14), a Jewish work, perhaps pre-Christian; and *The Testament of Hezekiah* (iii. 13–v. 1 *a*), which like *The Vision of Isaiah* (= vi.–xi.) is of Christian origin. The whole work appears to have been combined in its present form by a Christian editor, some time in the second century A.D.[1] The entire book is extant in an Ethiopic version, and fragments of it exist in Greek, Latin, and Slavonic. The original language in which the work was composed was certainly Greek for the two Christian parts, and probably also for the Jewish

[1] "From the third century onward the *Ascension* [in its present form] had an extensive circulation amongst Christian heretics" (Charles).

part (the *Martyrdom*), though this last may depend ultimately upon a Hebrew or Aramaic prototype.

The process by which these parts were fused into the present whole is difficult to determine exactly. According to Dr. Charles the complicated phenomena presented by the versions and fragments may be explained as follows. The last part, containing " the Vision of Isaiah " (vi.–xi.), was edited in two Greek recensions (G^1 and G^2). From G^2 a Latin (L^2) and a Slavonic (S) version were made. G^1 was united with the Greek texts (G) of the *Martyrdom* and the *Testament*, and the whole composite work so produced was translated into Ethiopic (E); fragments also are extant in Latin (L^1). The Greek text of G^1 is not extant, but it can be restored to a considerable extent from a Greek work, based upon it, which has survived, and is known as " the Greek Legend (of Isaiah)."[1] Another fragment of the Greek text, written on a papyrus of the fifth or sixth century, has been published by Grenfell and Hunt. It contains the text of ii. 4–iv. 4 (*i.e.* parts of the *Martyrdom* and *Testament*) and is denominated by Dr. Charles G^2, though it is not to be regarded as a distinct recension like the G^2 of the Vision (= vi.–xi.). All these texts (the Slavonic in a Latin translation) have been printed in parallel columns, and edited with critical notes, by Dr. Charles in his edition of our book (pp. 83–148).

In accordance with the critical analysis outlined above the whole work may be divided into four parts, and is so divided in the translation that follows.

---

[1] Discovered by Dr. O. von Gebhardt in a Greek MS. of the twelfth century, preserved in the National Library in Paris.

PART I. (= i. 1–iii. 12) contains the first part of *The Martyrdom of Isaiah*. Isaiah is introduced predicting, in the presence of Hezekiah and Jôsâb (*i.e.* Shear-jashub, Isaiah's son) his own death at the hands of Manasseh. After the death of Hezekiah, Isaiah, on account of the " lawlessness " and infamous practices of Manasseh, withdrew with certain other prophets into the desert in the neighbourhood of Bethlehem. Here he is pursued by Balchîrâ, a Samaritan, who denounces him to Manasseh, alleging that Isaiah had uttered prophecies against Jerusalem and the King, in whose heart Beliar dwells.

PART II. (=iii. 13–v. 1*a*) contains the so-called *Testament of Hezekiah* (iii. 13–iv. 18), a Christian writing. It has been introduced at this point by the Christian redactor to explain why Beliar is so much incensed with Isaiah. This was occasioned by Isaiah's prediction (here recorded) of the destruction of Sammael (Satan), the redemption of the world by Jesus, the founding of the Church, its persecution by Nero, which is the prelude to the final judgement. Incidentally a somewhat sombre picture is drawn of the state of affairs in the Church in these last days. Worldliness and lawlessness prevail among its ministers, there is much covetousness, respect of persons, slander and vainglory, and true " prophets " are hard to find. This picture reflects the state of affairs in the Church as it existed at the close of the first century, and harmonizes with similar accounts given in 2 Peter, 2 Timothy, and Clement of Rome (*ad Cor.* iii.).

PART III. (= v. 1*b*–14) contains the conclusion of the *Martyrdom*, resuming iii. 12. It recounts the story of Isaiah's martyrdom. The prophet is tempted by Balchîrâ to recant, but indignantly refusing to do so, is sawn asunder with a wooden saw.

PART IV. (= vi.–xi.) contains *The Vision of Isaiah*, a Christian writing. It describes a vision, which the prophet experienced while he was prophesying in the presence of King Hezekiah. While he was yet speaking he fell into a trance, with his eyes open. Afterwards he related the vision to the King and the prophets, but not to the people. The vision, as related, describes how the prophet was taken by an angel through the seven heavens, and what he saw there. In the seventh heaven he saw the departed righteous, including Abel and Enoch, and finally the Divine Being ("the Great Glory") Himself, together with a second glorious One like Him, and a third who is the Angel of the Holy Spirit. Then the Most High is heard commissioning the Son to descend through the heavens and the firmament to the world, and even to Sheol. The descent of "The Beloved" is then described, the birth of Jesus of a Virgin, His life, death, and resurrection, and the sending forth of the Twelve; and finally His Ascent though the seven heavens where He seats Himself on the right hand of "the Great Glory," the angel of the Holy Spirit being on the left. The prophet having related the vision to Hezekiah, warns him that these things will come to pass.

Dr. Charles thinks that the three independent writings, which form the constituent elements of our Book, were all, in their original form, in existence in the first century. This view is very probable. We have already seen that the picture of the state of affairs prevailing in the Church, given in the *Testament*, harmonizes with a first-century date.

INTRODUCTION

This seems to be true also of the last part (vi.–xi.). The Jewish colouring in both the Christian parts suggests a date not later than the end of the first century. On the other hand the *Martyrdom* may well be pre-Christian in substance.

TITLES OF THE BOOK

The book—or parts of it—is referred to in ancient patristic literature under various titles. Epiphanius terms the last part (vi.–xi.) " the Ascension of Isaiah " (τὸ Ἀναβατικὸν Ἡσαίου), as also does Jerome (" Ascensio Isaiae "); elsewhere it is referred to as " the Vision of Isaiah " (ὅρασις Ἡσαίου, " Visio Isaiae "), and this title is actually prefixed to chapter vi. in the texts of the Versions (" The Vision which Isaiah the son of Amoz saw "). Finally Georgius Cedrenus cites iv. 12, under the title of " the Testament of Hezekiah " (Διαθήκη Ἐζεκίου)—a title which, as Dr. Charles has shown, originally applied to an independent writing now incorporated in the entire work (= iii. 13–v. 1 *a*). As has already been mentioned, the Ethiopic version prefixes the title *The Ascension of Isaiah* to the whole composite work, and this is now the commonly accepted name of the entire book.

THE ANCIENT VERSIONS

The most important of the ancient versions is the Ethiopic (E), including as it does the entire text. It depends upon three MSS., two of which are in the British Museum, and one in the Bodleian Library at Oxford. The Ethiopic version was made, of course, from the Greek original, and according to Dr. Charles is " on the whole a faithful reproduction " of the first Greek Recension (G¹). An edition of the Ethiopic

INTRODUCTION

text was published by Archbishop Laurence in 1819, and an important critical one by Dillmann in 1877. Both these scholars also published translations of E. A Latin version of the last part of the *Ascension* (vi.–xi.) was printed at Venice in 1522 from a MS. now unknown. This is denominated by Dr. Charles L^2. Two fragments of what appears to be another Latin version, embracing ii. 14–iii. 13 and vii. 1–19, were discovered and edited by Mai in 1828. This version is styled by Dr. Charles L^1. Fortunately it is possible to compare L^1 and L^2 in a passage common to both, viz. vii. 1–19. When this is done it appears that L^1 and E agree, to a remarkable extent, against L^2 and the Slavonic (S). Hence Charles infers the existence behind them of two different recensions of the original Greek text (G), which he terms G^1 and G^2.[1] The combination EL^1 (and the " Greek Legend ") $= G^1$, and that of $SL^2 = G^2$. The arguments are given in full in Dr. Charles's edition, and appear to be convincing.

The Slavonic text, a Latin translation of which (by Prof. Bonwetsch) is given in Dr. Charles's edition, is a version of the last part only, the " Vision of Isaiah " (vi.–xi.). Its title is *The Vision which the [holy] Prophet Isaiah, the Son of Amoz, saw.* It is derived ultimately from two MSS. from which an edition by the Russian scholar, A. Popov, was published. As has been pointed out above it depends upon the recension of the original Greek text denominated G^2.

The text of the *Greek Legend*, which appears to have been based upon one of the recensions (G^1) of the original work is printed in full by Dr. Charles

[1] These were two recensions of the Greek text of vi.–xi.

INTRODUCTION xiii

in his edition of our book. The important papyrus fragment discovered by Grenfell and Hunt contains the Greek text of ii. 4–iv. 4. This is styled by Dr. Charles G^2, but must not be confounded with the G^2 which embraces vi.–xi, and is to be regarded as a distinct recension. Where the papyrus fragment differs from the text of EL^1 this difference, according to Dr. Charles, is to be explained " as due to the errors and variations incidental to the process of transmission " and not (as in the case of G^2 in vi.–xi.) as due to its being part of a distinct recension. The archetypal Greek text may still have been in existence in the fourth century.

SPECIAL IMPORTANCE OF THE BOOK

In accordance with the critical analysis we may regard our Book as containing three distinct and originally independent works, all of which go back to the first century. The last part reflects the beliefs, prevalent, in certain circles, on such subjects as the Trinity, the Incarnation, the Resurrection, the seven heavens, while the *Testament* (iii. 12–v. 1 *a*) gives a vivid picture of the state of affairs prevailing in the Christian Church at the close of the first century. It should be noted that both the Christian parts are apocalyptic in character, while the Jewish part—the *Martyrdom*—is a legendary narrative. This may well be of a much earlier date than the two Christian parts. For the legend which it embodies —Isaiah's death by being sawn asunder with a wooden saw—has very early attestation, and is not improbably alluded to in Heb. xi. 37 (*they were sawn asunder*). In fact the author of the Epistle to the Hebrews may very well have derived his knowledge

INTRODUCTION

of the legend from the *Martyrdom*. It is referred to clearly by Justin Martyr (*Trypho*, chap. cxx.), and constantly by later Christian writers. It is also attested in Jewish literature. Both Talmuds refer to Isaiah's death at the hands of Manasseh (cf. 2 Kings xxi. 16), and recount that Isaiah took refuge, fleeing from before Manasseh, in a cedar tree, and when this was discovered, Manasseh had the tree sawn asunder; and that as this was done the prophet's blood flowed out (cf. T.B. *Sanhedrin* 103^b, *Yebamoth* 49^b, T.J. *Sanhedrin* x). On the other hand the legend is not referred to explicitly by Josephus.

We may regard the *Martyrdom* as an early Jewish Midrash, based upon 2 Kings xxi. 16, and as perhaps composed or already in existence in the first half of the first century A.D. M. Halévy (*Études évangéliques* i. pp. 65 ff.), who accepts a pre-Christian date for the *Martyrdom*, has indeed tried to show that the narrative of Our Lord's Temptation has been influenced by it. But his parallels are not very convincing. The relevant passage in the Martyrdom (v. 4–8) may be allowed to speak for itself. It runs as follows:

And Balchîrâ said to Isaiah: "*Say: I have lied in all that I have spoken, and likewise the ways of Manasseh are good and right: and the ways also of Balchîrâ and of his associates are good.*" *And this he said to him when he began to be sawn in sunder. But Isaiah was (absorbed) in a vision of the Lord, and though his eyes were open, he saw them (not).*

And Balchîrâ spake thus to Isaiah: "*Say what I say unto thee and I will turn their heart, and I will compel Manasseh and the princes of Judah and all the people and all Jerusalem to reverence thee.*"

And Isaiah answered and said: "*So far as I have*

utterance (*I say*) : *Damned and accursed be thou and all thy powers and all thy house. For thou canst not take (from me) aught save the skin of my body.*"

This rather bald and jejune account is remote, both in substance and spirit, from the sublime narrative in the Gospels. To suggest anything like direct dependence of the latter on the former, or to regard the Jewish account as the " source " of the Gospel narrative is surely far-fetched. Nevertheless the *Martyrdom* sheds some interesting light on the Jewish demonology current in the first century. Thus Beliar (=Belial) appears as one of the names of the Prince of evil spirits (= Satan). He is " the Angel of lawlessness, who is the ruler of this world " (cf. John xii. 31; xvi. 11; 2 Cor. iv. 4; Ephes. vi. 12). He is in many respects like *Sammael*—also a satanic being—though possibly, as Charles suggests, Sammael is regarded as subordinate to Beliar, executing the latter's behests (i. 8). The origin and significance of the name Beliar (Belial) is a matter of controversy; but it seems clear that it had mythological associations, and may originally have been a designation of the underworld (Sheol, Hades) into which the living descend at death, and from which there is no return (= *Bal-ya'al*, " there is no ascent "). This seems to be the meaning of the term in Ps. xviii. 5:

The breakers of Death had come about me, and the streams of Belial affrighted me:

Here *Belial* is parallel to *Death* = place of death, *i. e.* Sheol.[1] Another illuminating passage, in this connection, is Ps. xli. 8:

A matter of Belial [*Hades*] (*i. e.* a mortal disease) *is fixed upon him*,

---

[1] *Death* and *Sheol* are often parallel; cf. *e.g.* Is. xxviii. 15, 18.

And now that he lieth he will rise up no more.

The personification easily follows. *Death* and *Sheol* were so personified (cf. Ps. xviii. 6), becoming names of the prince of the underworld, and in exactly the same way Belial (Beliar) becomes the name of the prince of evil powers. For a New Testament parallel cf. 2 Cor. vi. 15 (*What concord hath Christ with Belial?*). Beliar is also designated expressly by another mysterious name. *Matanbûchûs* (cf. ii. 4, "Beliar whose name is Matanbûchûs"). The commonly accepted explanation of this bizarre form is that it is composed of two Hebrew words, *mattan bûḳâ*, meaning "worthless gift." But this is not very satisfactory. Halévy suggests that it is really a form of the Hebrew *mithdabek*, "one who attaches himself," and so designates the evil spirit as the possessor of its victim. There is some support for this explanation in a passage of the Talmud (T.B. *Shabbāth* 32ª) where, according to one reading of the text, the woman who neglects certain duties is spoken of as threatened by three "mortal possessions" ("attachments of death"), *i.e.* mortal diseases, which Rashi *ad loc.* explains as so called "because they attach and bring close death before its time." The "one who takes possession" is an admirable designation of the evil spirit, and harmonizes well with the representation which depicts Beliar as "dwelling" "in the heart of Manasseh" (iii. 11).[1] It should be added that Belial (Beliar) appears in the *Book of Jubilees* in a Satanic *rôle*. He is represented as the accuser and father of all idolatrous nations (*Jub.* i. 20). In the *Testaments*

---

[1] Kohler, in *J.E.* ii. 659, suggests that Metembûchûs may be a "corrupt form" of *Angro-mainyush* or Ahriman, the evil deity of the religion of Ancient Persia.

INTRODUCTION xvii

of the Twelve Patriarchs Belial is depicted as the archfiend, the head of the evil spirits, and the source of impurity and lying.

Another demonic figure that appears in the *Martyrdom* is Sammael (= " venom of God "), who occupies an important place in the late Jewish literature both Talmudic and post-Talmudic. In this literature he is represented as prince of the demons, and is identified with the angel of death, who slays men with a drop of poison. He is " the chief of the Satans " (*Deut. rabb.* xi. 9; cf. Matt. ix. 34, " the prince of the devils "), and plays the part of accuser, seducer, and destroyer. He thus seems to be identical with Beliar (Belial), but in the *Martyrdom* he is apparently subordinated to the latter (cf. i. 8). In i. 8 he is surnamed *Malchîrâ*, which may possibly be explained, as Halévy suggests, as = " king of evil " (*melek* or *malki ra'*), or " messenger of evil " (*mal'ak ra'*). Perhaps the name of the Samaritan false prophet, *Balchîrâ*, who takes so active a part in bringing about the prophet's martyrdom, may also be explained as = " chosen of evil " (*behîr-ra'*). According to Dr. Charles' analysis the name " Sammael " was originally peculiar to the *Martyrdom* (i. 8, 11; ii. i), though it also occurs in editorial additions (vii. 9; iii. 13; v. 15, 16; xi. 41). In the last of these passages Sammael is identified with Satan (" Sammael Satan "). It should be added that Beliar is entirely absent from the " vision " (vi.–xi.). He appears, however, in the *Testament*, but not, as in the *Martyrdom*, as a purely immaterial spirit, but as incarnate in Nero, thus fulfilling the *rôle* of Antichrist (" the Beliar Antichrist," iv. 2, 14, 16, 18). In exactly the same way in the Sibyllines

iv. 2[1] Belial (Beliar) descends from heaven as Antichrist, and appears as Nero, the slayer of his mother. This conception is important for the history of the Antichrist idea. Ultimately the idea may be derived from the early myth of a terrible conflict waged with the Dragon of Chaos—Tiamat—by the divine Hero, who eventually overcomes her. Here, very probably, we have the prototype of the later Antichrist legend, which has undergone so remarkable and rich a development in the course of the ages. On the principle which plays so important a *rôle* in eschatological development, that " Urzeit " = " Endzeit " —the last stage will reproduce the first—the transference of the idea of the mythical combat of the divine Hero with the primæval Dragon to the end of the ages is easy to understand. The conception thus arises of the battle of God with the devil at the end of the world. " It is very likely," says Bousset,[2] " that Antichrist is originally nothing else than the incarnate devil, and that the idea of a battle of God with a human opponent, in whom all devilish wickedness would become incarnate, arose under the influence of definite historical conditions." The first historical figure to be identified with Antichrist was the persecutor of the Jews, the Syrian King Antiochus Epiphanes, whose lineaments are depicted in the Book of Daniel, and who became the type of the God-opposing tyrant. Later, as in the middle section of our Book (the *Testament*) and in the Book of Revelation, it was Nero.[3] Later still, it was discovered now

---

[1] Of Christian origin.   [2] Art. *Antichrist* (*E.R.E.* i. 578 f.).
[3] In the Psalms of Solomon (first century B.C.), Pompey the Great, the violator of the Holy of Holies, is the Antichrist. He is referred to as " the dragon " (ii. 29) and the " sinner " (ii. 1). For the Neronic Antichrist in *Revelation*, cf. Rev. xvii.

in this, now in that historical character. But it must not be forgotten that the political application of the idea, though it assumed a dominating place in the later development, was not an essential or original feature of the conception. Occasionally, as in 2 Thess. ii. 3 f.—where " the man of lawlessness " = Beliar, and " he that opposeth and exalteth himself against all that is called God " = Antichrist, *i. e.* the combined phrase = Beliar-Antichrist—the Antichrist, freed from political associations, becomes a purely ideal figure which works in the spiritual sphere.

A striking feature of our Book is the designation of the Messiah as " The Beloved." This Messianic title is found in all parts of the Book, though, according to Charles it was originally peculiar to the two Christian parts, viz. to the *Testament* (iii. 13, 17, 18; iv. 3, 6, 9, 18), and the *Vision* (vii. 17, 23; viii. 18, 25; ix. 12). The passages in the *Martyrdom* where it occurs (i. 4, 5, 7, 13) are, he thinks, due to the final editor. There are good grounds, as Dr. Armitage Robinson has shown,[1] for believing that this title is pre-Christian. It is used in the Old Testament as a title of Israel (ὁ ἠγαπημένος LXX); cf. *e. g.* Deut. xxxii. 15, xxxiii. 5, 26, where it is the Greek rendering of *Jeshurun* (cf. also Is. xliv. 2); the terms ὁ ἠγαπημένος and ὁ ἀγαπητός also occur in Is. v. 1, 7. The transference of the title from the people as a whole to the Messiah was, therefore, perfectly natural, as the parallel cases of " Servant " and " Elect " show. Further, at the time when the Gospels were written the terms " Beloved " and " Elect " were practically interchangeable, for St. Matthew (xii. 18) writes " my

[1] Hastings, *D.B.*, ii. 501.

Beloved" (ὁ ἀγαπητός μου), in citing Is. xlii. 1, where the Hebrew has "mine Elect," and conversely St. Luke (ix. 35), in the narrative of the Transfiguration, substitutes "Chosen" ("Elect") (ὁ ἐκλελεγμένος) for "Beloved" (Mark ix. 7). It should be added that in the phrase ὁ υἱός μου ὁ ἀγαπητός (Mark i. 11; ix. 7), ὁ ἀγαπητός is probably to be regarded as a separate title, and the rendering should be "My Son, the Beloved." The title is used also as a synonym for "Christ" in Eph. i. 6 ("his grace which he freely bestowed on us in the Beloved"), and is freely employed as a designation of Christ in early Christian writings (Ep. Barn., Clem. Rom., Ignatius, Hermas), and certain passages in the LXX where ὁ ἀγαπητός occurs were interpreted Messianically by Christian writers (*e. g.* Ps. xliv. [xlv] title, Zech. xii. 10). Its frequent use in our Book as a stereotyped term for the Messiah is thus an interesting link in the evidence for the gradual establishment of its use in this sense.

Turning now to the *Vision* (vi.–xi.), we find some interesting and important features which call for comment. In ch. vii. foll. the visionary experience of the prophet is described, how he was conducted by the angel through the seven heavens, and what he saw there. We have here an elaborate description of the seven heavens, which in fulness can only be paralleled with the well-known one in the *Slavonic Enoch*.[1] The conception of a plurality of heavens was widespread in the ancient world, and was probably known to the ancient Babylonians, and certainly to the followers of Zoroaster, as well as to certain Greek philosophers in the West. It can be

---

[1] Cf. the elaborate discussion in Charles' ed. of the Slavonic Enoch, pp. xxx.–xlvii.

INTRODUCTION xxi

traced in the Old Testament, in the apocalyptic and New Testament writings, in the Talmud, and in early Christian literature (outside the New Testament). Ultimately it was given up by Christian theology, and was even banned as heretical. The particular conception of *seven* heavens seems to be due ultimately to astral theories. The sevenfold division of the planets gave birth to the sevenfold division of earth and hell in ancient Babylonian thought, and it is exceedingly probable that this division was applied to the heavens also in ancient Babylonian religion.

In the Old Testament the conception of a plurality of the heavens is probably implicit in the Hebrew term for " heaven " (*shāmayîm*) which is plural in form. It comes to explicit expression in such phrases as " the heaven of heavens " (Deut. x. 14; 1 Kings viii. 27; Ps. cxlviii. 4), and the idea that Satan has access there to the very presence of God (Job i., ii.; cf. 1 Kings xxii. 19–22) may possibly point in the same direction.

It is, however, in the apocalyptic literature of Judaism that the conception is most fully elaborated. One of the fullest descriptions is found in the *Test. XII Patriarchs* (Levi ii. 7 f.). Here, however, as Charles and other scholars have shown, there are traces of redaction, and it is probable that the earliest (and original) form of the passage was a description of *three* heavens, and that this was transformed later by redaction into a description of the seven. Thus the earliest Hebrew idea of a plurality of Heavens, seems to have been that there were *three*, and this idea may underlie the Old Testament passages enumerated above. But by the beginning of the Christian era and subsequently the doctrine of seven heavens was firmly established in Judaism. A detailed description, as has been said, is given of them in the *Slavonic Enoch* (first century A.D.), and it may underlie the description of the seven " ways " or stages apportioned to souls after death in 4 Ezra vii. 90–98 (end of first century A.D.). From Jewish it passed over to Christian apocalypses such as our Book. In the Babylonian Talmud (*Ḥag.* 12^b) there is a discussion of this subject, and the doctrine that there are seven heavens is associated with the name of Resh Laḳish (*c.* 260 A.D.). It is there reported—

Resh Laḳish said: There are seven (heavens), and these be they: *Vilon* (= *velum*, " *curtain* "), *Raḳîa'*, *Shĕḥaḳîm, Zĕbûl, Mā'ôn, Mākhôn, 'Arābôth.*

It is worth noting that in the detailed description of the seven heavens given in the *Slavonic Enoch* a place in one of them (the third) is reserved for the damned. (*Slav. Enoch* x.), and in the second are the fallen angels (ch. vii.).

When we turn to the New Testament we find clear traces of the same conception. St. Paul (2 Cor. xii. 2 f.) explicitly mentions " the third heaven " as the place of location of Paradise, which agrees with the representation of the *Slavonic Enoch*. It has been disputed whether St. Paul's conception embraced only three or seven heavens. But in view of the evidence of the *Slavonic Enoch* it seems probable that the later and more developed view lies at the background of his thought. Similarly in the Epistle to the Ephesians (i. 3, 20; ii. 6; iii. 10; and vi. 12) the remarkable phrase is used " in the heavenly (places) " or " sphere " (ἐν τοῖς ἐπουρανίοις), which certainly points in the same direction. It is remarkable that the presence of evil (evil powers) " in the heavenly sphere" is here explicitly recognized (cf. Ephes. vi. 12, "against the spiritual hosts of wickedness in the heavenly sphere"). We may also compare, in this connection, Col. i. 20: "to reconcile all things unto Himself, whether things upon the earth or things in the heavenly sphere." By "the things in the heavenly sphere" are meant probably either the fallen angels imprisoned in the second heaven, or "the powers of Satan whose domain is in the air" (cf. also Ephes. iii. 10). Christ is represented as having "ascended far above all the heavens" (cf. also Heb. iv. 14; vii. 26); and in Rev. xii. "war" in heaven is spoken of, Michael and his angels warring against Satan and his host, who are overthrown and expelled. This last feature gives expression to the religious feeling that found the presence of evil in heaven intolerable.

It can, of course, be argued, and with a considerable amount of truth, that this language of St. Paul and the other New Testament writers must not be unduly pressed. It is a striking fact that nowhere in the New Testament do we find a detailed or materialistic description of the heavenly sphere such as we meet with in some of the earlier apocalyptic writings. There is a marked absence of painful literalism. The dominant ideas behind the language are essentially spiritual. It is, no doubt, largely symbolical. Nor must it be forgotten that the tendency to spiritualize the old crude conception is marked in the late Jewish Apocalypse of Ezra (4 Ezra), the composition of which may be dated about 100 A.D. Nevertheless, even if this be so, it is obvious that the detailed doctrine is implied, and that in its fully developed form it had secured a firm place in first-century

INTRODUCTION

Judaism. This conclusion is confirmed by our Book. The part with which we are at present concerned, viz. the "Vision" (vi.–xi.) was, at the earliest, composed at the latter end of the first century A.D., and probably by a Jewish Christian. It seems not improbable that the detailed account of the seven heavens here given has been influenced by the *Slavonic Enoch*. The description in our Book is, perhaps, less crude and materialistic, but obviously the conception was very much alive in certain (?Jewish and Jewish Christian) circles at the end of the first century A.D. Another point of contact between the two writings may be seen in the idea of heavenly "garments" with which the righteous will be clothed, the "garments" being the spiritual bodies which are awaiting them in heaven (cf. vii. 22; viii. 14, 26; ix. 9, 17, 24–26; xi. 40; also iv. 16). According to the *Slavonic Enoch* (xxii. 8–10) these "garments" of the blessed are to be composed of God's glory. The New Testament parallels to this idea are referred to in the notes.

A word must be said in conclusion about the very important passage, xi. 2–22, which gives the circumstances of Christ's birth of the Virgin Mary, and emphasizes the Virgin-Birth. Several scholars, including Dillmann and Schürer, regard this section as an interpolation, and for this view there is some positive ground in the fact that the section is substantially absent from the old Latin Version and the Slavonic, which omit all references to Mary and Joseph and Christ's birth. Nevertheless, the section is probably a genuine part of the original work, as Charles rightly argues from the internal evidence. The elimination of all reference to the circumstances of the Birth may easily be explained as due to dogmatic reasons in the interests of a Docetic view of Christ. The Book certainly had an extensive circulation among heretics, and the Latin Version was preserved in these circles. We may add that it would be very extraordinary if, in a Christian writing of the latter part of the first century, which purports to narrate the vision of Isaiah about Christ and His descent from heaven to earth, no mention was made of His birth of a Virgin. The famous passage, Is. vii. 14, had received a Christian application in Jewish Christian circles, as Matt. i. shows. It is incredible that this Jewish-Christian application of the sense was unknown to the writer of the " Vision " at the end of the first century, and it would have been impossible for him to have ignored it. In any case this important section is an early attestation of the doctrine. It should be noted also that the passage, even in its complete form, reveals traces of incipient Docetism. The birth is represented as having taken place without any natural pangs. Doubtless the elimination of all reference to the birth came later, in order to satisfy the demands of the full-blown Docetic theory. The conception of the Trinity is also interesting. The Son and the Holy Spirit are worshipped (ix. 27–36), but they also worship God (ix. 39–40); and the Holy Spirit is referred to as an angel (" the Angel of the Spirit " or " the Angel of the Holy Spirit "). This representation seems also to be characteristically Jewish Christian.

BIBLIOGRAPHY

The works of Laurence and Dillmann have already been referred to. The most complete and important edition of the Book both for the texts of the versions, translation, interpretation and criticism is that of Dr. Charles : *The Ascension of Isaiah* (London, 1900).[1]

Dillmann's text has also been translated into French by Basset : *Les Apocryphes Éthiopiens*, iii., *L'Ascension d'Isaïe* (1894).

An important study of the *Martyrdom* has been published by the Jewish scholar, J. Halévy, in his *Études évangéliques* (Paris, 1903), pp. 65 ff.

Reference may also be made to the articles *Isaiah, Ascension of*, in Hastings' *D.B.* (by Dr. Armitage Robinson, important), in *J.E.* and in Wace's *Dictionary of Christian Biography.* Schürer has discussed questions of Introduction in § 32, vi. of his *History of the Jewish People in the Time of Christ*, and gives a conspectus of the passages in the patristic literature which refer to our Book. In the corresponding section of the last German edition a full and up-to-date Bibliography is given.

---

[1] An edition of the *Martyrdom* (only), by Charles, is included in the Oxford *Apocrypha and Pseudepigrapha*, ii. 155-162. In the German *Die Apokryphen und Pseudepigraphen*, ed. by Kautzsch, an edition of the *Martyrdom* (only) is included (by Beer).

SHORT TITLES, SYMBOLS AND BRACKETS USED IN THIS EDITION

1 Enoch = the Ethiopic Book of Enoch.

2 Enoch = the Slavonic Book of Enoch.

Ap. Bar. = the Syriac Apocalypse of Baruch.

G denotes the lost Greek archetype of $G^1 G^2$.

G^1 denotes the lost Greek text from which EL^1 were translated, and on which the Gk. Leg. was based.

G^2 denotes the Greek text from which SL^2 were translated, of which ii. 4–iv. 2 has now been recovered.

E denotes the Ethiopic Version.

S denotes the Slavonic Version.

L^1 denotes the Latin Version from G^1 (consisting of ii. 14–iii. 13; vii. 1–19).

L^2 denotes the Latin Version from G^2 (consisting of vi.–xi.).

⌜ ⌝. The use of these brackets in the English translation of E means that the words so enclosed are found in G^1 and not in G^2. In certain cases the words peculiar either to G^1 or G^2 are derived from G.

( ). The words or letters so enclosed are supplied by the editor.

* *. The words so enclosed are emendations of the text.

† †. The words so enclosed are corrupt.

[ ]. The words so enclosed are interpolated.

D.B. = *Dictionary of the Bible*, and *E.R.E.* = *Encyclopædia of Religion and Ethics*. Both edited by Dr. Hastings.

J.E. = *Jewish Encyclopædia*.

Presumed additions by the final editor of the whole composite work are indicated in the text of the translation by italic type.

THE ASCENSION OF ISAIAH

PART I

The Martyrdom of Isaiah[1] (I. 1–III. 12).

I. 1. And it came to pass in the twenty-sixth year of the reign of Hezekiah king of Judah that he called Manasseh his son. Now he was his only one. 2. And he called him into the presence of Isaiah the son of Amoz the prophet, and into the presence of Jôsâb[2] the son of Isaiah, *in order to deliver unto him the words of righteousness which the king himself had seen:* 3. *And of the eternal judgements and the torments of Gehenna*[3] *and of the *prince* of this world,*[4] *and of his angels, and his authorities and his powers,* 4. *And the words of the faith of the Beloved*[5] *which he himself had seen in the fifteenth year*[6] *of his reign during his illness.* 5. *And he delivered unto him the written words which Samnas the scribe had written*[7] *and also those which Isaiah, the*

---

[1] The extracts from the Jewish *Martyrdom of Isaiah* are contained (with certain editorial additions indicated by italic type) in i. 1–iii. 12+v. 1b–14. Between these sections the *Testament of Hezekiah* (iii. 13b–iv. 18) is inserted.

[2] *Jôsâb* = (*Shear*)-Jashub; cf. Is. vii. 3.

[3] *Gehenna:* cf. iv. 14 (not again in this book).

[4] *Prince of this world*, i. e. Beliar; cf. ii. 4; iv. 2; x. 29.

[5] i. e. the Messiah, a title frequently occurring in this book (and probably pre-Christian in this sense).

[6] Cf. 2 Kings xx. 1–6; Is. xxxviii. 1–20.

[7] *Samnas* = Shebna (so vi. 17); verses 5b–6 are a summary description of the Vision of Isaiah contained in chaps. vi.–xi.

son of Amoz, had given to him, and also to the prophets, that they might write and store up with him what he himself had seen in the king's house regarding the judgement of the angels,[1] *and the destruction of this world, and regarding the garments of the saints and †their† going forth, and regarding †their† transformation and the persecution and ascension of the Beloved.* 6. *In the twentieth year of the reign of Hezekiah, Isaiah had seen the words of this prophecy and had delivered them to Jôsâb his son.* And whilst he (Hezekiah) gave commands, Jôsâb the son of Isaiah standing by, 7. Isaiah said to Hezekiah the king, but not in the presence of Manasseh only did he say unto him: "As the Lord liveth, whose name hath not been sent into this world, and as the Beloved of my Lord liveth, and the Spirit which speaketh in me [2] liveth, all these commands and these words will be made of none effect by Manasseh thy son, and through the agency of his hands I shall depart mid the torture of my body. 8. And Sammael Malchîrâ [3] will serve Manasseh, and execute all his desire, and he will become a follower of Beliar [4] rather than of me: 9. And many in Jerusalem and in Judæa he will cause to abandon the true faith, and Beliar will dwell in Manasseh, and by his hands I shall be

---

[1] The Messiah will judge the angels; cf. iv. 18, x. 12; according to one view the saints will act as the Messiah's assessors at the judgement, cf. 1 Cor. vi. 3 (1 Thess. iii. 13).

[2] The Holy Spirit speaks through the prophets; cf. ix. 36.

[3] Sammael, originally one of the chief archangels, tempted Eve, and became the chief of the Satans and the angel of death: see further *J.E.* x. 665 f. (art. *Sammael*. For Malchira cf. Introduction, p. xvii.).

[4] *Beliar* later identified with Satan (in the Sibyllines with Antichrist). See Introduction, p. xv ff.

sawn asunder." 10. And when Hezekiah heard these words he wept very bitterly, and rent his garments, and placed earth upon his head, and fell on his face. 11. And Isaiah said unto him : " The counsel of Sammael against Manasseh is consummated : nought will avail thee." 12. And on that day Hezekiah resolved in his heart to slay Manasseh his son. 13. And Isaiah said to Hezekiah : " The Beloved hath made of none effect thy design, and the purpose of thy heart will not be accomplished, *for with this calling have I been called and I shall inherit the heritage of the Beloved.*"

II. 1. And it came to pass after that Hezekiah died and Manasseh became king, that he did not remember the commands [1] of Hezekiah his father but forgat [2] them, and Sammael abode in Manasseh and clung fast to him. 2. And Manasseh forsook the service of the God of his father, and he served Satan and his angels and his powers. 3. And he turned aside the house of his father which had been before the face of Hezekiah (from) the words of wisdom and from the service of God. 4. And Manasseh turned aside his heart to serve Beliar; for the angel of lawlessness, who is the ruler [3] of this world, is Beliar, whose name is Matanbûchûs.[4] And he delighted in Jerusalem because of Manasseh, and he made him strong in apostatizing (Israel) and in the lawlessness which was spread abroad

---

[1] Cf. i. 6. 7.

[2] *forgat*, a play on the name *Manasseh* (in Hebrew); cf. Gen. xli. 51.

[3] *ruler of this world is Beliar :* cf. x. 29; John xii. 31, xvi. 11 (*prince of this world*); 2 Cor. iv. 4 (*god of this world*); Ephes. vi. 12.

[5] *Matanbûchûs*, meaning uncertain—possibly = "worthless gift" (Lücke) : but cf. Introduction, p. xvi.

in Jerusalem. 5. And witchcraft [1] and magic increased, and divination and auguration, and fornication, [and adultery], and the persecution [2] of the righteous by Manasseh and [Belachîrâ, and] Tobia the Canaanite,[3] and John of Anathoth,[3] and by (Zadok) the chief of the works.[3] 6. And the rest of the acts, behold they are written in the book of the Kings of Judah and Israel. 7. And, when Isaiah, the son of Amoz, saw the lawlessness which was being perpetrated in Jerusalem and the worship of Satan and his wantonness, he withdrew from Jerusalem and settled in Bethlehem of Judah. 8. And there also there was much lawlessness, and withdrawing from Bethlehem he settled on a mountain in a desert place. 9. And Micaiah [4] the prophet, and the aged Ananias, and Joel and Habakkuk, and his son Jôsâb, and many of the faithful *who believed in the ascension into heaven*, withdrew and settled on the mountain. 10. They were all clothed with garments of hair,[5] and they were all prophets. And they had nothing with them, but were naked, and they all lamented with a great lamentation because of the going astray of Israel. 11. And these ate nothing save wild herbs [6] which they gathered on the mountains, and having cooked them, they lived thereon together

---

[1] *witchcraft*, etc.: cf. 2 Kings xxi. 6.
[2] Cf. 2 Kings xxi. 16.
[3] Unknown.
[4] *And Micaiah*, etc., cf. vi. 7. "The aged Ananias" may possibly be Hanani, father of Jehu, a prophet: cf. 1 Kings xvi. 1–7.
[5] Cf. Matt. iii. 4.
[6] Cf. 4 Ezra ix. 26; Dan. x. 2, 3. Such asceticism was one of the most esteemed ways of preparing for the reception of a divine revelation.

with Isaiah the prophet. And they spent two years of days on the mountains and hills. 12. And after this, whilst they were in the desert, there was a certain man in Samaria named Belchîrâ, of the family of Zedekiah, the son of Chenaan,¹ a false prophet, whose dwelling was in Bethlehem. Now †Hezekiah † ² the son of Chanânî, who was the brother of his father, and in the days of Ahab, king of Israel, had been the teacher of the 400 prophets of Baal,³ had himself smitten ⁴ and reproved Micaiah the son of Amâdâ the prophet. 13. And he, Micaiah, had been reproved by Ahab and cast into prison. (And he was) with Zedekiah the prophet : they were with Ahaziah the son of *Ahab, king in Samaria.* 14. And Elijah the prophet of Têbôn ⁵ of Gilead was reproving Ahaziah and Samaria, and prophesied ⁶ regarding Ahaziah that he should die on his bed of sickness, and that Samaria should be delivered into the hand of Leba Nâsr ⁷ because he had slain the prophets of God. 15. And when the false prophets, who were with Ahaziah the son of Ahab and their teacher Jâlerjâs of Mount †Joel†, had heard—16. Now he was a brother of Zedekiah—when they had heard, they persuaded Ahaziah the king of †Aguarôn † ⁸ and (slew) Micaiah.

¹ For this false prophet cf. 1 Kings xxii. 11.
² Apparently a mistake for Zedekiah (*i.e.* the same person as the one just before mentioned). This Zedekiah was an uncle of Belchirâ.
³ Cf. 1 Kings xviii. 22 (confused here with 1 Kings xxii. 6).
⁴ Cf. 1 Kings xxii. 24 (Micaiah, son of Imlah, in 1 Kings).
⁵ *Têbôn* = Thisbe, a town of Naphtali; cf. 1 Kings xvii. 1, where " of the sojourners of " is taken by LXX as = " οἱ Thesbe."
⁶ Cf. 2 Kings i. 1-6.
⁷ Corrupt for Salmanassar.
⁸ Read *Gomorrha* with the Latin.

III. 1. *And Belchîrâ* recognized and saw the place of Isaiah and the prophets who were with him; for he dwelt in the region of Bethlehem, and was an adherent of Manasseh. And he prophesied falsely in Jerusalem, and many belonging to Jerusalem were confederate with him, and he was a Samaritan. 2. And it came to pass when Alagar Zagâr,[1] king of Assyria, had come and captured Samaria and taken the nine (and a half) tribes[2] captive, and led them away to the *mountains* of the Medes and the rivers of Tâzôn;[3] 3. This (Belchîrâ), whilst still a youth, had escaped and come to Jerusalem in the days of Hezekiah king of Judah, but he walked not in the ways of his father of Samaria; for he feared Hezekiah. 4. And he was found in the days of Hezekiah speaking words of lawlessness in Jerusalem. 5. And the servants of Hezekiah accused him, and he made his escape to the region of Bethlehem. And *they*[4] persuaded . . . 6. And Balchîrâ accused Isaiah and the prophets who were with him, saying: "Isaiah and those who are with him prophesy against Jerusalem and against the cities of Judah that they shall be laid waste, and (against the children of Judah and) Benjamin also that they shall go into captivity, and also against thee, O Lord the king, that thou shalt go (bound) with hooks and iron chains:" 7. But they prophesy falsely against Israel and Judah. 8. And Isaiah himself hath said: "I see more than Moses the prophet." 9. But Moses

[1] Read *Salmanassar* with the Latin.
[2] *i.e.* the (northern) Kingdom of Israel; cf. 4 Ezra xiii. 40, and *Ap. Bar.* lxii. 5, etc.
[3] *i.e.* Gozan: cf. 2 Kings xvii. 6; xviii. 11.
[4] *i.e.*? the false prophets; the missing object may be *Balchîrâ* (Grenfell and Hunt).

said : " No man can see God and live " ;[1] and Isaiah hath said : " I have seen God and, behold, I live."[2] 10. Know, therefore, O king, that *he is lying*. And Jerusalem also he hath called Sodom, and the princes of Judah and Jerusalem he hath declared to be the people of Gomorrah.[3] And he brought many accusations against Isaiah and the prophets before Manasseh. 11. But Beliar dwelt in the heart of Manasseh and in the heart of the princes of Judah and Benjamin and of the eunuchs and of the councillors of the king. 12. And the words of Belchirâ pleased him [exceedingly], and he sent and seized Isaiah.

PART II (iii. 13–v. 1a)

The Testament of Hezekiah (iii. 13b–iv. 18).

13. For Beliar was in great wrath against Isaiah by reason of the vision, and because of the exposure wherewith he had exposed Sammael, and because through him the going forth of the Beloved from the seventh heaven had been made known, and His transformation and His descent and the likeness into which He should be transformed, (that is) the likeness of man, and the persecution wherewith He should be persecuted, and the tortures wherewith the children of Israel should torture Him, and the coming of His twelve disciples, and the teaching, and that He should before the Sabbath be crucified upon the tree, and should be crucified together with wicked men, and that He should be buried in the sepulchre. 14. And the twelve who were with Him should be offended because of Him :[4] and *the watch of* those who watched the

---

[1] Ex. xxxiii. 20. [2] Is. vi. 1. [3] Cf. Is. i. 10. [4] Matt. xxvi. 31.

sepulchre : [1] 15. And the descent of the angel of the Christian Church,[2] which is in the heavens, whom He will summon in the last days. 16. And that (Gabriel) the angel of the Holy Spirit,[3] and Michael, the chief of the holy angels, on the third day will open the sepulchre : 17. And the Beloved sitting on their shoulders will come forth and send out His twelve disciples : 18. And they will teach all the nations [4] and every tongue of the resurrection of the Beloved, and those who believe in His cross [5] will be saved, and in His ascension into the seventh heaven whence He came : 19. And that many who believe in Him will speak through the Holy Spirit : 20. And many signs and wonders will be wrought in those days. 21. And afterwards, on the eve of His approach, His disciples will forsake the teaching of the Twelve Apostles, and their faith, and their love and their purity.[6] 22. And there will be much contention [7] on the eve of [His advent and] His approach. 23. And in those days many will love office, though devoid of wisdom. 24. And there will be many lawless elders, and shepherds dealing wrongly by their own sheep, and they will ravage (them) owing to their not *having* holy shepherds. 25. And many will change the honour of the garments of the saints for the garments of the covetous,[8] and there will be much respect of persons in those days and lovers of the honour of this world. 26. And there will be much slander and vainglory at the approach of the Lord, and the Holy Spirit will withdraw

---

[1] Cf. Matt. xxviii. 4.   [2] Cf. Rev. ii. 1, 8, etc.
[3] Cf. iv. 21; vii. 23; ix. 36, 39, 40; x. 4; xi. 4, 33. The phrase usually means the Holy Spirit.
[4] Cf. Matt. xxviii. 19.   [5] Cf. ix. 26.   [6] Cf. 1 Tim. iv. 12.
[7] Cf. 1 Tim. iv. 1; 2 Pet. ii. 1.   [8] Cf. 2 Tim. iii. 1, 2.

from many. 27. And there will not be in those days many prophets, nor those who speak trustworthy words, save one here and there in divers places, 28. On account of the spirit of error [1] and fornication and of vainglory, and of covetousness, which shall be in those, who will be called servants of that One [2] and ·in those who will receive that One. 29. And there will be great hatred in the shepherds and elders towards each other. 30. For there will be great jealousy in the last days; for every one will say what is pleasing in his own eyes. 31. And they will make of none effect the prophecy of the prophets which were before me,[3] and *these* my visions also will they make of none effect, in order to speak after the impulse of their own heart.

IV. 1. And now Hezekiah and Jôsâb my son, *these* are the days of the *completion of the world*. 2. After it is consummated, Beliar the great ruler, the king of this world, will descend, who hath ruled it since it came into being; yea, he will descend from his firmament [4] in the likeness of a man, a lawless king, the slayer of his mother : [5] who himself (even) this king 3. Will persecute the plant [6] which the Twelve Apostles of the Beloved have planted. Of the Twelve one will be delivered into

[1] Cf. 1 John iv. 6.
[2] *i. e.* The Beloved.
[3] The false teachers repudiate the Old Testament. This rather suggests Gnostic teachers.
[4] As distinct from the first heaven above it.
[5] The allusion seems to be to Nero, who is identified with Antichrist : cf. *Sib. Or.* iv. 121; v. 145, 363, etc. For Antichrist as " the man of lawlessness," cf. 2 Thess. ii. 3 (R.V. *marg.*).
[6] *i. e.* the Church. For " plant of righteousness "=Israel: cf. 1 Enoch xciii. 5.

THE ASCENSION OF ISAIAH [CHAP. IV

his hands.[1] 4. This ruler in the form of that king will come and there will come with him all the powers of this world,[2] and they will hearken unto him in all that he desireth. 5. And at his word the sun will rise at night and he will make the moon to appear at the sixth hour.[3] 6. And all that he hath desired he will do in the world : he will do and speak like the Beloved and he will say : " I am God and before me there hath been none." [4] 7. And all the people in the world will believe in him. 8. And they will sacrifice to him and they will serve him saying : " This is God and beside him there is no other." [5] 9. And the greater number of those who shall have been associated together in order to receive the Beloved, he will turn aside after him.[6] 10. And there will be the power of his miracles in every city and region. 11. And he will set up his image [7] before him in every city. 12. And he shall bear sway three years and seven months and twenty-seven days.[8] 13. And many believers and saints having seen [9] Him for whom they were hoping, who was crucified, Jesus the Lord Christ, [after that I, Isaiah, had seen Him who was crucified and ascended] and those also who were believers in Him—of these

---

[1] *i. e.* probably St. Peter, who, with St. Paul, suffered martyrdom in the Neronian persecution (64–65 A.D.).

[2] Cf. Rev. xx. 7–9; xvi. 14.

[3] Cf. 4 Ezra v. 4 (2 Thess. ii. 9; Rev. xiii. 14; xix. 20).

[4] Cf. 2 Thess. ii. 4 (Rev. xiii. 5 f.).

[5] Cf. Rev. xiii. 4, 8, 12.

[6] Cf. Matt. xxiv. 24; Mark xiii. 22.

[7] Cf. Rev. xiii. 14. Images of the Roman Emperor were set up in various cities to be worshipped.

[8] *i. e.* 1335 days = Dan. xii. 12. The last period of three and a half years marks the reign of Antichrist.

[9] *i. e.* personally (cf. John xx. 29); this points to the first century.

CHAP. IV]　　　　　PART II　　　　　　　39

few in those days will be left [1] as His servants, while they flee [2] from desert to desert, awaiting the coming [3] of the Beloved. 14. And after (one thousand) three hundred and thirty-two [4] days the Lord will come with His angels and with the armies of the holy ones [5] from the seventh heaven with the glory of the seventh heaven, and He will drag Beliar into Gehenna [6] and also his armies. 15. And He will give rest [7] to the godly whom He shall find in the body [8] in this world,[9] [and the sun will be ashamed] : 16. And to all who because of (their) faith in Him have execrated Beliar and his kings.[10] But the saints will come with the Lord [11] with their garments [12] which are (now) stored up on high in the seventh heaven : with the Lord they will come, whose spirits are clothed,[13] they will descend and be present in the world,[14] and He will strengthen those who have been found in the body, together with the saints,[15] in the garments of the saints, and the Lord will minister to those who have kept watch in

[1] Cf. Luke xviii. 8.
[2] *i.e.* from before the Antichrist; cf. Mark xiii. 14 f.; Rev. xii. 6, 14.
[3] Cf. 1 Cor. i, 7; Phil. iii. 20, etc.
[4] ? read thirty-five (1335 days); see iv. 12.
[5] *i.e.* the angels; cf. 2 Thess. i. 7; Jude 14; 1 Enoch i, 4, 9.
[6] Cf. Rev. xix. 20.
[7] *i.e.* refreshment; cf. Acts iii. 19.
[8] Cf. 1 Thess. iv. 17.
[9] According to some apocalyptic writers they must be gathered in Palestine in order to secure the Messianic salvation; cf. 4 Ezra ix. 8; xiii. 48.
[10] Cf. Rev. xvii. 12–13.
[11] Cf. 1 Thess. iii. 13; iv. 14.
[12] Cf. Rev. iii. 4, 5, 18; iv. 4; vi. 11, etc.
[13] *i.e.* with spiritual bodies; cf. 1 Cor. xv. 44.
[14] This is the first resurrection (of certain saints) : cf. Rev. xx. 1–6.
[15] *i.e.* the glorified saints who had descended.

this world. 17. And afterwards they[1] will turn themselves upward in their garments, and their body will be left in the world. 18. Then the voice of the Beloved will in wrath rebuke the things of heaven and the things of earth and the mountains and the hills and the cities and the desert and the forests and the angel of the sun[2] and that of the moon, and all things wherein Beliar manifested himself and acted openly in this world, and there will be [a resurrection and] a judgement in their midst in those days, and the Beloved will cause fire[3] to go forth from Him, and it will consume all the godless,[4] and they will be as though they had not been created. 19. *And the rest of the words of the vision are written in the vision of Babylon.*[5] 20. *And the rest of the vision regarding the Lord, behold, it is written in the parables according to my words which are written in the book which I publicly prophesied.* 21. *And the descent of the Beloved into Sheol, behold, it is written in the section, where the Lord saith: "Behold, my Son will understand."*[6] *And all these things, behold they are written [in the Psalms] in the parables*[7] *of David, the son of Jesse, and in the Proverbs of Solomon his son, and in the words of Korah, and Ethan the Israelite, and in the words of Asaph, and in the rest of the Psalms also which the angel of the Spirit inspired,* 22. (*Namely*) *in those which have not the*

---

[1] *i.e.* the saints found alive on the earth.
[2] Cf. Rev. xix. 17, and (for the other angels mentioned) 1 Enoch lx. 12–21; Rev. vii. 1, 2; xiv. 18. *Jubilees* ii.
[3] Cf. 2 Thess. i. 8; ii. 8 (Is. xi. 4).
[4] Cf. 4 Ezra xii. 33; xiii. 38, 49.
[5] Cf. Is. xiii. 1 (LXX).
[6] *i.e.* Is. lii. 13 (LXX). Perhaps the Descent was supposed to be referred to in Is. liii. 8 (Charles).
[7] " Parables," *i.e.* songs.

name written,[1] *and in the words of my father Amoz and of Hosea the prophet, and of Micah and Joel and Nahum and Jonah and Obadiah and Habakkuk and Haggai and Zephaniah and Zechariah and Malachi, and in the words of Joseph the Just* [2] *and in the words of Daniel.*

PART III (v. 1-14)

The Martyrdom of Isaiah (v. 1b-14) resumed from iii. 12).

V. 1. *On account of these visions, therefore, Beliar was wroth with Isaiah, and he dwelt in the heart of Manasseh* and he sawed him in sunder with a wooden saw. 2. And when Isaiah was being sawn in sunder Balchîrâ stood up, accusing him, and all the false prophets stood up, laughing and rejoicing because of Isaiah. 3. And Balchîrâ, with the aid of Mechêmbêchûs,[3] stood up before Isaiah, [laughing] deriding; 4. And Balchîrâ said to Isaiah :[4] " Say : ' I have lied in all that I have spoken, and likewise the ways of Manasseh are good and right. 5. And the ways also of Balchîrâ and of his associates are good.' " 6. And this he said to him when he began to be sawn in sunder. 7. But Isaiah was (absorbed) in a vision of the Lord, and though his eyes were open, he saw them (not). 8. And Balchîrâ spake thus to Isaiah : " Say what I say unto thee and I will turn their heart, and I will compel Manasseh and the princes of Judah and the people and all Jerusalem to reverence

[1] *viz.* those psalms with no ascription of authorship (*e.g.* Pss. i. and ii.).
[2] Probably a pseudepigraphic work entitled *The Prayer of Joseph*, only known from a few citations : see Hastings, *D.B.* ii. 778.
[3] Cf. ii. 4 (note) = ? *Matanbûchûs*, i. e. Beliar.
[4] Verses 4-8 contain the Temptation of Isaiah by Balchîrâ.

thee. 9. And Isaiah answered and said: " So far as I have utterance (I say) : Damned and accursed be thou and all thy powers [1] and all thy house. 10. For thou canst not take (from me) aught save the skin of my body." 11. And they seized and sawed in sunder Isaiah, the son of Amoz, with a wooden saw. 12. And Manasseh and Balchîrâ and the false prophets and the princes and the people [and] all stood looking on. 13. And to the prophets who were with him he said before he had been sawn in sunder : " Go ye to the region of Tyre and Sidon ; for for me only hath God mingled the cup.[2] 14. And when Isaiah was being sawn in sunder, he neither cried aloud nor wept, but his lips spake with the Holy Spirit until he was sawn in twain. 15. *This Beliar did to Isaiah through Balchîrâ and Manasseh ; for Sammael was very wrathful against Isaiah from the days of Hezekiah, king of Judah, on account of the things which he had seen regarding the Beloved,* 16. *And on account of the destruction of Sammael, which he had seen through the Lord, while Hezekiah his father was still king. And he did according to the will of Satan.*

PART IV

The Vision of Isaiah (vi. 1–xi. 43).

THE VISION WHICH ISAIAH THE SON OF AMOZ SAW.

VI. 1. In the twentieth year of the reign of Hezekiah, king of Judah, came Isaiah the son of Amoz,

---

[1] Balchîrâ is here addressed by Isaiah as a personification of Beliar.
[2] For the figure of the cup in this connection cf. Mark x. 38; xiv. 36, and parallels.

and Jôsâb, the son of Isaiah, to Hezekiah to Jerusalem ⌐from Galgalâ¬. 2. And (having entered) he sat down on the couch of the king, ⌐and they brought him a seat, but he would not sit (thereon)¬. 3. ⌐And when Isaiah began to speak the words of faith and truth with King Hezekiah¬, all the princes of Israel were seated and the eunuchs and the councillors of the king. And there were there ⌐forty¬ prophets and sons of the prophets: they had come from the villages and from the mountains and the plains when they had heard that Isaiah was coming from Galgalâ to Hezekiah. 4. ⌐And they had come¬ to salute him ⌐and to hear his words. 5. And that he might place his hands upon them,¬ and that they might prophesy and that he might hear their prophecy: ⌐and they were all before Isaiah.¬ 6. And when Isaiah was speaking ⌐to Hezekiah¬ the words of truth and faith, they all heard †a door which one had opened and†[1] the voice of the Holy Spirit. 7. And the king summoned all the prophets and all the people who were found there, and they came. And Micaiah and the aged Ananias and Joel ⌐and Jôsâb¬ sat on his right hand (and on the left). 8. And it came to pass when they had all heard the voice of the Holy Spirit, they all worshipped on their knees, and glorified the God ⌐of truth¬, the Most High ⌐who is in the upper world and who sitteth on high the Holy One and¬ who resteth among His holy ones.[2] 9. ⌐And they gave glory to Him¬ †who had thus bestowed a door in an alien world, had bestowed (it)

---

[1] *A door*, etc. The text of verse 6 seems to be corrupt. Perhaps we should read with the Latin (L²): *Then he spake words of truth; the Holy Spirit came upon him, and all saw and heard words of the Holy Spirit.*

[2] Cf. Is. lvii. 15 (LXX).

on a man†.[1] 10. And as he was speaking in the Holy Spirit in the hearing of all, he became silent ⌜and his mind was taken up from him⌝ and he saw not [2] the men that stood before him, 11. Though his eyes, indeed, were open. Moreover, his lips were silent ⌜and the mind in his body was taken up from him.⌝ 12. But his breath was in him; ⌜for he was seeing a vision.[3] 13. And the angel who was sent to make him see was not of this firmament,[4] nor was he of the angels of glory of this world, but he had come from the seventh heaven.⌝ 14. And the people who stood near did (not) think, but †the circle of the prophets (did)†,[5] that the holy Isaiah had been taken up. 15. And the vision which the holy Isaiah saw was not from this world but from the world which is hidden from the flesh. 16. And after Isaiah had seen this vision, he narrated it to Hezekiah, and to Jôsâb his son ⌜and to the other prophets who had come. 17. But the leaders and the eunuchs and the people did not hear, but only Samna [6] the scribe, and †Ijôaqêm, and† [7] Asaph the recorder; for these also were doers of righteousness, and the †sweet smell† [8] of the Spirit was upon them. But the people had not heard; for Micaiah and Jôsâb his son had caused them to go forth, when the wisdom of this world had been taken from him and he became as one dead.

---

[1] *who had thus bestowed*, etc. Text corrupt: read with Charles *who had thus bestowed such excellence of words on a man in the world*.
[2] Cf. v. 7.   [3] A description of the ecstatic state.
[4] The abode of Beliar; cf. iv. 2.
[5] Corrupt: read *The prophets recognized*.
[6] = *Samnas* (i. 5), *i. e.* Shebna.
[7] ? read *Joah the son of (Asaph)*; cf. Is. xxxvi. 3 (Charles).
[8] or *good pleasure* (= εὐδοκία) : so Charles.

VII. 1. And the vision which Isaiah saw, he told to Hezekiah and Jôsâb his son⌐ and Micaiah and the rest of the prophets, (and) said : 2. *At this moment*, when I prophesied according to the (words) heard which ye heard, I saw a glorious angel not like unto the glory of the angels which I used always to see, but possessing such glory and †position† that I cannot describe ⌐the glory⌐ ⌐of that angel⌐. 3. And having seized me by my hand *he raised me on high*, and I said unto him : " Who art thou, and what is thy name, and whither art thou raising me on high ? " For strength was given me to speak with him. 4. And he said unto me : " When I have raised thee on high [through the (various) degrees] and made thee see the vision, on account of which I have been sent, then thou wilt understand who I am : but my name thou dost not know : 5. Because thou wilt return into this thy body, but whither I am raising thee on high, thou wilt see ; ⌐for for this purpose have I been sent."⌐ 6. And I rejoiced because he spake courteously to me. 7. And he said unto me : " Hast thou rejoiced because I have spoken courteously to thee ? " And he said : " And thou wilt see how a greater also than I am will speak courteously and peaceably with thee. 8. And †His Father also who is greater†[1] thou wilt see ; for for this purpose have I been sent from the seventh heaven in order to explain all these things unto thee." 9. And we ascended to the firmament, I and he,[2] and there I saw Sammael and his hosts, and there was great fighting therein,

---

[1] Read *One more eminent man the Greater Himself* (Charles).
[2] Cf. the ascent of Abraham and the angel, and the meeting with Azazel, in *Ap. Abraham*, ch. xii. foll.

and the *angels* of Satan were envying one another.
10. And as above so on the earth also; for the likeness of that which is in the firmament is here on the earth. 11. And I said unto the angel (who was with me) : " (What is this war and) what is this envying? " 12. And he said unto me : " So hath it been since this world was made until now, and this war (will continue) till He, whom thou shalt see will come and destroy him. 13. And afterwards he caused me to ascend (to that which is) above the firmament : which is the (first) heaven. 14. And there I saw a throne [1] in the midst, and on his right and on his left were angels. 15. ⌜And (the angels on the left were) not like unto the angels who stood on the right⌝,[2] but those who stood on the right had the greater glory, and they all praised with one voice, ⌜and there was a throne [3] in the midst⌝, and those who were on the left gave praise after them; but their voice was not such as the voice of those on the right, nor their praise like the praise of those. 16. And I asked the angel who conducted me, and I said unto him : " To whom is this praise sent? " 17. And he said unto me : " (It is sent) to the praise of (Him who sitteth in) the seventh heaven : to Him †who resteth in the holy world†,[4] and to His Beloved, whence I have been sent to thee. [Thither is it sent.]" 18. And again he made me to ascend to the second heaven. Now the height of that heaven is the same as from the heaven to the earth

---

[1] ? " an angel belonging to the order called ' Thrones ' " (Charles); cf. Col. i. 16; Test. Lev. iii. 8.

[2] For the superiority of right to left, cf. vii. 29, 30, 33, 34, and see further *J.E.* x. 419 f. (art. *right and left*).

[3] *i. e.* ? an angel.

[4] = ? *to Him who inhabiteth eternity* (Is. lvii. 15) : cf. vi. 8.

[and to the firmament]. 19. And (I saw there, as) in the first heaven, angels on the right and on the left, ⌜and a throne in the midst, and the praise of the angels in the second heaven; and he who sat on the throne in the second heaven was more glorious than all (the rest).⌝ 20. And there was great glory in the second heaven, and the praise also was not like the praise of those who were in the first heaven. 21. And I fell on my face to worship him,[1] but the angel who conducted me did not permit me, but said unto me: "Worship neither throne nor angel which belongeth to the six heavens—for for this cause I was sent to conduct thee—until I tell thee ⌜in the seventh heaven⌝. 22. For above all the heavens and their angels hath thy throne been placed, and thy garments[2] and thy crown which thou shalt see." 23. And I rejoiced with great joy, that those who love the Most High and His Beloved will afterwards ascend thither by the angel of the Holy Spirit. 24. And he raised me to the third heaven, and in like manner I saw those upon the right and upon the left, and there was a throne there in the midst; but the memorial of this world is there unheard of. 25. ⌜And I said to the angel who was with me;⌝ for the glory of my appearance was undergoing transformation as I ascended to each heaven in turn: "Nothing ⌜of the vanity⌝ of that world is here named." 26. And he answered me, and said unto me: "Nothing is named on account of its weakness, and nothing is hidden there of what is done." 27. ⌜And I wished to learn how it is known, and he answered me saying: "When I have raised thee to the seventh heaven whence I was sent, to that which is above these,

[1] Cf. Rev. xix. 10; xxii. 8, 9.   [2] Cf. iv. 16.

then thou shalt know that there is nothing hidden from the thrones and from those who dwell in the heavens and from the angels." ⁿ And the praise wherewith they praised and the glory of him who sat on the throne was great, ᶠand the glory of the angels on the right hand and on the left was beyond that of the heaven which was below themⁿ. 28. And again he raised me to the fourth heaven, and the height from the third to the fourth heaven was greater than from the earth to the firmament. 29. And there again I saw those who were on the right hand and those who were on the left, ᶠand him who sat on the throne (who) was in the midstⁿ, and there also they were praising. 30. And the praise and glory of the angels on the right was greater than that of those on the left. 31. And again the glory of him who sat on the throne was greater than that of the angels on the right, and their glory was beyond that of those who were below. 32. And he raised me to the fifth heaven. 33. And again I saw ᶠthose upon the right hand and on the left, and him who sat on the throne possessing greater glory than those of the fourth heavenⁿ. 34. And the glory of those on the right hand was greater than that of those ᶠon the left [from the third to the fourth]. 35. And the glory of him who was on the throne was greater than that of the angels on the right handⁿ. 36. And their praise was more glorious than that of the fourth heaven. 37. ᶠAnd I praised Him, who is not named and the Only-begottenⁿ [1] who dwelleth in the heavens, whose name is not known to any flesh, who hath bestowed such glory on the several heavens, ᶠand who maketh great the glory of the angels, and

[1] Cf. John i. 16, 18; iii. 16, 18.

more excellent the glory of Him who sitteth on the throne⌐.

VIII. 1. And again he raised me into the air of the sixth heaven, and I saw such glory as I had not seen in the five heavens. 2. *For I saw* angels possessing great glory. 3. And the praise there was holy and wonderful. 4. And I said to the angel who conducted me: "What is this which I see, my Lord?" 5. And he said: "I am not thy lord, but thy fellow-servant."[1] ⌐6. And again I asked him, and I said unto him: "Why are there not angelic fellow-servants (on the left)?"⌐ 7. And he said: "From the sixth heaven there are no longer *angels* on the left, nor a throne set in the midst, but (they are directed) by the power of the seventh heaven, where dwelleth He that is not named[2] ⌐and the Elect One, whose name hath not been made known, and none of the heavens can learn His name⌐.[3] 8. For it is He alone to whose voice all the heavens and thrones give answer. I have ⌐therefore been empowered and⌐ sent to raise thee here that thou mayest see this glory. 9. And that thou mayest see the Lord of all those heavens and these thrones, 10. ⌐Undergoing (successive) transformation until He resembleth your form and likeness.⌐ 11. I indeed say unto thee, Isaiah; No man about to return into a body of that world hath ⌐ascended or⌐ seen what thou seest or perceived what thou hast perceived and what thou wilt see. 12. For it hath been permitted to thee in the lot of the Lord to come hither[4] [and from thence cometh the power of the sixth heaven and of the air]." 13. And I

---

[1] Cf. Rev. xix. 10; xxii. 8, 9. [2] *i. e.* The Ineffable.
[3] Cf. Rev. ii. 17; xix. 12.   [4] *i. e.* the seventh heaven.

magnified my Lord with praise, in that through His lot I should come hither. 14 And he said: "⌜Hear, furthermore, therefore, this also from thy fellow-servant⌝; when from the body by the *will of God* thou hast ascended hither, then thou wilt receive the garment [1] ⌜which thou seest, and likewise other numbered garments laid up (there) thou wilt see⌝, 15. And then thou wilt become equal to the angels of the seventh heaven." 16. And he raised me up into the sixth heaven, and there were no (angels) on the left, nor a throne in the midst, but all had one appearance [2] and their (power of) praise was equal. 17. And (power) was given to me also, and I also praised along with them and that angel also,[3] and our praise was like theirs. 18. And there they †all named the primal Father† and His Beloved, ⌜the Christ⌝ and the Holy Spirit, all with one voice. 19. And (their voice) was not like the voice of the angels in the five heavens, 20. [Nor like their discourse] but the voice was different there, and there was much light there. 21. And then, when I was in the sixth heaven I thought the light which I had seen in the five heavens to be but darkness.[4] 22. And I rejoiced and praised Him who hath bestowed such lights on those who wait for His promise. 23. And I besought the angel who conducted me that I should not henceforth

[1] Cf. viii. 26; ix. 9, 24, 25; xi. 3, 5.
[2] Cf. 2 Enoch xix. 1.
[3] Cf. *Ap. Abraham* xvii., where Abraham and the conducting angel join in a song of praise in heaven.
[4] The light referred to is no doubt the uncreated light of the Divine Glory, which is a well-known feature in the Midrashic literature; cf. also *Ap. Abraham*, ch. xvii.; Rev. xxi. 23; xxii. 5. [But this light has its centre in the seventh heaven; cf. verse 25 a few lines lower down.]

return to the carnal world. 24. I say indeed unto you, ⌜Hezekiah and Jôsâb my son and Micaiah⌝ that there is much darkness here. 25. And the angel who conducted me discovered what I thought, and said : " If in this light thou dost rejoice, how much more wilt thou rejoice, when in the seventh heaven thou seest the light, where is the Lord and His Beloved [whence I have been sent, who is to be called ' Son ' in this world. 26. Not (yet) hath been manifested He who shall be in the corruptible world] [1] and the garments, and the thrones, and the crowns which are laid up for the righteous, ⌜for those who trust in that Lord who will descend in your form. For the light which is there is great and wonderful⌝. 27. And as concerning thy not returning into the body thy days are not yet fulfilled for coming here." 28. And when I heard (that) I was troubled, and he said : " Do not be troubled."

IX. 1. And he took me into the air of the seventh heaven, and moreover I heard a voice saying : " How far will he ascend that dwelleth *in the flesh*? " and I feared and trembled. 2. And ⌜when I trembled, behold⌝ *I heard* from hence [2] another voice ⌜being sent forth, and⌝ saying : " It is permitted to the holy Isaiah to ascend hither, for here is his garment." 3. And I asked the angel who was with me ⌜and said⌝ : " Who is he who forbade me and who is he who *permitted* me to ascend? " 4. And he said unto me : " He who forbade thee, this is he *who is over* the praise-giving of the sixth heaven. 5. And He who *permitted* thee, this is ⌜thy Lord God, the Lord Christ, who will

---

[1] Omit bracketed words (Charles).
[2] rather, *from above*, i. e. from the seventh heaven.

be called ' Jesus ' in the world⌐, but His name¹ thou canst not hear till thou hast ascended out of thy body." 6. And he raised me up into the seventh heaven, and I saw there a wonderful light and angels innumerable. 7. And there I saw all the righteous ⌐from the time of Adam. 8. And there I saw the holy Abel and all the righteous. 9. And there I saw Enoch and all who were with him⌐, stript of the garments of the flesh, and I saw them in their garments of the upper world, and they were ⌐like angels⌐,² standing there in great glory. 10. But they sat not on their thrones,³ nor were their crowns⁴ of glory on them. 11. And I asked the angel who was with me : " How is it that they have received the garments, but have not the thrones and the crowns?" 12. And he said unto me : 13. " Crowns and thrones of glory they do not receive, till the Beloved will descend in the form in which you will see Him descend ⌐[will descend, I say] into the world in the last days the Lord, who will be called Christ⌐. Nevertheless, they ⌐see and⌐ know whose will be thrones, and whose the crowns when He hath descended, and been made in your form, ⌐and they will think that He is flesh and is a man⌐. 14. And the god of that world will stretch forth *his hand against the Son,* and they will crucify Him on a tree, and will *slay* Him not knowing who He is. 15. And thus His descent, ⌐as you will see, will be hidden even from the heavens, so that it will not

---

¹ *i. e.* His heavenly name; cf. Rev. xix. 12, and see viii. 7 of this book.
² Cf. Matt. xxii. 30; *Ap. Bar.* li. 5, 12.
³ Cf. Rev. iii. 21; Luke xxii. 29, 30; Matt. xix. 28.
⁴ *i. e.* as victors; cf. Rev. ii. 10; iii. 11; iv. 4; Jas. i. 12; 2 Tim. iv. 7, 8.

be known who He is⁷. 16. And when He hath plundered the angel of death,[1] He will ascend on the third day, [and he will remain in that world five hundred and forty-five days].[2] 17. And then many of the righteous will ascend [3] with Him, whose spirits do not receive their garments [4] till the ⌐Lord Christ⌐ ascend [5] and they ascend with Him. 18. Then, indeed, they will receive their [garments and] thrones and crowns, when He hath ascended into the ⌐seventh⌐ heaven. 19. And I said unto him that which I had asked him in the third heaven : 20. " *Show me how* everything which is done in that world is here made known." 21. And whilst I was still speaking with him, behold one of the angels who stood nigh, more glorious than the glory of that angel who had raised me up from the world, 22. Showed me a book, [but not as a book of this world] and he opened it, and the book was written, but not as a book of this world.[6] And he gave (it) to me and I read it, and lo ! the deeds of the children of Israel were written therein, and the deeds of those whom *I* know (not), my son Jôṣâb. 23. And I said : " In truth, there is nothing hidden in the seventh heaven, which is done in this world." 24. And I saw there many garments laid up, and many thrones and many crowns. 25. And I said to the angel :

---

[1] The " harrowing of Hell " was effected, according to the Latin *Gospel of Nicodemus* (Part ii.) by the descent of Christ into Hades; cf. Rev. xx. 13 (Matt. xxvii. 52 f.).

[2] A Gnostic interpolation (Charles).

[3] *viz*. from Hades.

[4] *i.e.* their spiritual bodies.

[5] *viz*. to heaven.

[6] *i.e.* one of the heavenly books; these were to be opened at the judgement; cf. Dan. vii. 10; cf. also in the N.T., Rev. iii. 5; xiii. 8; xvii. 8, and often (" the book of life ").

"Whose are these garments and thrones and crowns?" 26. And he said unto me: "These garments many from that world will receive, believing in the words of That One, ⌜who shall be named⌝ as I told thee, ⌜and they will observe those things, and believe in them, and believe in His cross: for them are *these* laid up⌝." 27. And I saw a certain One [1] ⌜standing, whose glory surpassed that of all,⌝ and His glory was great ⌜and wonderful. 28. And after I had seen Him,⌝ all the righteous whom I had seen ⌜and also the angels whom I had seen⌝ came to Him. ⌜And Adam and Abel and Seth, and all the righteous first drew near⌝ and worshipped Him, and they all praised Him with one voice, ⌜and I myself also gave praise with them,⌝ and my giving of praise was as theirs. 29. And then all the angels drew nigh and worshipped and gave praise. 30. And *I* was (again) transformed [2] and became like an angel. 31. And thereupon the angel who conducted me, said to me: "Worship this One," and I worshipped and praised. 32. And the angel said unto me: "This is the Lord of all the praisegivings which thou hast seen." 33. And whilst *he* was still speaking, I saw another Glorious One [3] who was like Him, and the righteous drew nigh and worshipped and praised, and I praised together with them. But *my* glory was not transformed into accordance with their form. 34. And thereupon the angels drew near and worshipped Him. 35. And I saw the Lord and the second angel, and they were standing. 36. And the second whom

[1] Christ is meant. Note the emphasis laid on the worship of Him in heaven.
[2] Cf. vii. 25. Isaiah underwent successive transformations.
[3] The Third Person of the Godhead (Charles).

I saw was on the left of my Lord. And I asked: "Who is this?" and he said unto me: "Worship Him, for He is the angel of the Holy Spirit, who *speaketh* in thee and the rest of the righteous." 37. And I saw the great glory, the eyes of my spirit being open, and I could not thereupon see,[1] nor yet could the angel who was with me, nor all the angels whom I had seen worshipping my Lord. 38. But I saw the righteous [2] beholding with great power the glory of that One. 39. And my Lord drew nigh to me and the angel of the Spirit ⌜and He said: "See how it is given to thee to see God, and on thy account power is given to the angel who is with thee." 40. And I saw how my Lord and the angel of the Spirit⌝ worshipped, and they both together praised ⌜God⌝. 41. And thereupon all the righteous ⌜drew near and⌝ worshipped. 42. And the angels ⌜drew near and⌝ worshipped and all the angels praised.

X. 1. And thereupon I heard the voices and the giving of praise, which I had heard in each of the six heavens, ascending *and being heard* there: 2. And all ⌜were being sent up to that Glorious One⌝ whose glory I could not behold. 3. ⌜And I myself was hearing and beholding the praise (which was given) to Him. 4. And the Lord and the angel of the Spirit were beholding all and hearing all⌝. 5. And all the praises which are sent up from the six heavens [3] are not only heard but seen. 6. And ⌜I heard⌝ the angel ⌜who conducted me and⌝ he said: "This is the Most High of the high ones, dwelling

---

[1] *saw . . . could not see:* i.e. saw for a moment, but could not steadfastly behold. By "the Great Glory," is meant the First Person: cf. 1 Enoch xiv. 20.

[2] *i.e.* the glorified righteous; cf. Rev. xxii. 4.

[3] Cf. vii. 16–17.

in the holy world,¹ and resting in His holy ones, who will be called by the Holy Spirit through the lips of the righteous ⌜the Father of the Lord⌝." 7. And I heard the voice of the Most High ⌜the Father of my Lord⌝ saying to my Lord ⌜Christ who will be called Jesus⌝ : 8. " Go forth and descend through all the heavens, and Thou wilt descend to ⌜the firmament and⌝ that world : to the angel in Sheol ² Thou wilt descend, ⌜but to Haguel ³ Thou wilt not go⌝. 9. And Thou wilt become like unto the likeness of all who are in the five heavens. 10. ⌜And Thou wilt be careful to become like the form of the angels of the firmament [and the angels also who are in Sheol]⌝. 11. And none of the angels of that world shall know ⁴ ⌜that Thou art Lord with Me of the seven heavens and of their angels. 12. And they shall not know that Thou art with Me, *till* with a *loud* voice ⁵ I have called (to) the heavens, and their angels and their lights, (even) unto the sixth heaven, in order that Thou mayst⌝ judge ⌜and destroy⌝ the †princes† and angels ⌜and gods⌝ of that world,⁶ and the world that is dominated by them : 13. For they have denied Me and said : ' We alone are, and there is none beside us.' ⁷ 14. And afterwards from the *angels* of death Thou wilt ascend to Thy place, and Thou wilt not be transformed in each heaven, but in glory wilt Thou ascend and sit on My right hand. 15. And thereupon the princes and powers

---

¹ Based on Is. lvii. 15 (LXX); cf. vi. 8.
² *Sheol* = Hades : and " the Angel in Sheol " = the Angel of Death.
³ *Haguel* = Abaddon or Gehenna (the abode of the lost).
⁴ Cf. 1 Cor. ii. 8.
⁵ *viz.* at the day of Judgement.
⁶ Cf. John xvi. 11.
⁷ Cf. Is. xlvii. 8.

†of that world† will worship Thee." ¹ 16. These commands I heard the Great Glory giving to my Lord. 17. And †so† I saw my Lord go forth from the seventh heaven into the sixth heaven. 18. And the angel who conducted me [from this world was with me and] said unto me : " Understand, Isaiah, and see how the transformation and descent of the Lord *will appear*." 19. And I saw, and when the angels saw Him, ⌜thereupon those in the sixth heaven⌝ praised and lauded Him; for He had not been transformed after the shape of the angels there, ⌜and they praised Him⌝ and I also praised with them. 20. And I saw when He descended into the fifth heaven, that in the fifth heaven He made Himself like unto the form of the angels there, and they did not praise Him (nor worship Him); for His form was like unto theirs. 21. And then He descended into the fourth heaven, and made Himself like unto the form of the angels there. 22. And ⌜when they saw Him⌝, they did not praise ⌜or laud Him⌝; for His form was like unto their form. 23. And again I saw when He descended into the third heaven, ⌜and He made Himself like unto the form of the angels in the third heaven. 24. And those who kept the gate of the (third) heaven demanded the password,² and the Lord gave (it) to them in order that He should not be recognized. And when they saw Him, they did not praise or laud Him; for His form was like unto their form. 25. And again I saw when He descended⌝ into the second heaven, ⌜and again He gave the password ² there; those who kept the gate proceeded to demand and the Lord to give. 26. And I saw when He made Himself like unto the

---

¹ Cf. Heb. i. 6.   ² or *sign*.

form of the angels in the second heaven, and they saw Him and they did not praise Him; for His form was like unto their form. 27. And, again, I saw when He descended⌐ into the first heaven, ⌐and there also He gave the password [1] to those who kept the gate, and He made Himself like unto the form of the angels who were on the left of that throne⌐, and they neither praised nor lauded Him; for His form was like unto their form. ⌐28. But as for me no one asked me on account of the angel who conducted me⌐. 29. And again He descended into the firmament ⌐where dwelleth the ruler of this world⌐, and He gave the password [1] ⌐to those on the left⌐, and His form was like theirs, and they did not praise Him there; ⌐but they were envying one another and fighting; for here there is a power of evil and envying about trifles⌐. 30. And I saw when He descended ⌐and made Himself like⌐ unto the angels of the air, and He was like one of them. 31. And He gave no password; [1] ⌐for one was plundering and doing violence to another.⌐

XI. 1. After this ⌐I saw, and ⌐the angel ⌐who spoke with me, who conducted me⌐, said unto me : " Understand, Isaiah, son of Amoz; for for this purpose have I been sent from God." 2. [2] ⌐And I, indeed, saw a woman of the family of David [3] the prophet, named Mary, a Virgin, and she was espoused to a man named Joseph, a carpenter, and he also was of the seed and family of the righteous David of Bethlehem

---

[1] or *sign*.

[2] xi. 2–22 are wanting in the Latin version (L²) and in the Slavonic. But the whole section appears to be original.

[3] The Davidic descent of the Virgin Mary is here explicitly asserted. This belief has very early attestation; cf. Justin Martyr, *Trypho* c. xliii., xlv., c. etc.

Judah. 3. And he came into his lot. And when she was espoused, she was found with child, and Joseph the carpenter was desirous to put her away.[1] 4. But the angel of the Spirit appeared in this world, and after that Joseph did not put her away, but kept Mary and did not reveal this matter to any one. 5. And he did not approach Mary, but kept her as a holy virgin, though with child. 6. And he did not live with her for two months. 7. And after two months of days while Joseph was in his house, and Mary his wife, but both alone—8. It came to pass that when they were alone Mary straightway looked with her eyes and saw a small babe, and she was astonied.[2] 9. And after she had been astonied, her womb was found as formerly before she had conceived. 10. And when her husband Joseph said unto her : " What has astonied thee ? " his eyes were opened and he saw the infant and praised God, because into his portion God had come. 11. And a voice came to them : " Tell this vision to no one."[3] 12. And the story regarding the infant was noised abroad in Bethlehem. 13. Some said : " The Virgin Mary hath borne a child before she was married two months." 14. And many said : " She hath not borne a child, nor hath a midwife gone up (to her), nor have we heard the cries of (labour) pains." And they were all blinded respecting Him and they all knew regarding Him, though they knew not whence He was.[4] 15. And they took Him, and went to Nazareth in Galilee. 16. And I saw, O Hezekiah and Jôsâb my son, and I declare to the other prophets also who are standing by, that (this)

[1] Cf. Matt. i. 20 f.   [2] Cf. *Protev. Jaccbi* xix.
[3] Cf. *op. cit.* xx. (end).   [4] Cf. John vii. 27.

hath escaped all the heavens and all the princes and all the gods of this world.¹ 17. And I saw: In Nazareth He sucked the breast as a babe and as is customary in order that He might not be recognized. 18. And when He had grown up He worked great signs and wonders in the land of Israel and of Jerusalem. 19. And after this the adversary envied Him and roused the children of Israel against Him⌐, not knowing who He was, ⌐and they delivered Him to the king, and crucified Him, and He descended to the angel (of Sheol). 20. In Jerusalem, indeed, I saw Him being crucified on a tree: 21. And likewise after the third day rise again and remain days. 22. And the angel who conducted me said: " Understand, Isaiah : " and I saw when He sent out the Twelve Apostles ² and ascended⌐. 23. And I saw Him, and He was in the firmament, but He had not changed Himself into their form, and all the angels of the firmament ⌐and the Satans⌐ saw Him ³ and they worshipped. 24. And ⌐there was much sorrow there, while⌐ they said : " How did our Lord descend *in our midst*, and we perceived not the glory [which hath been upon Him], which we see hath been upon Him from the sixth heaven ? " 25. And He ascended into the second heaven, and He did not transform Himself, but all the angels who were on the right and on the left and the throne in the midst 26. Both worshipped Him and praised Him and said : " How did our Lord escape us whilst descending, and we perceived not ? " 27. And in like manner He

---

¹ Cf. Ignatius *ad Ephes.* xix.: *And hidden from the prince of this world were the virginity of Mary, and her child-bearing, and likewise also the death of the Lord:* cf. also 1 Cor. ii. 7, 8.

² Cf. iii. 17; Matt. xxviii. 18 f.; Acts i. 8 f.

³ *all the angels . . . saw Him:* cf. 1 Tim. iii. 16.

ascended into the third heaven, ⌜and they praised and said in like manner.⌝ 28. And in the fourth heaven and in the fifth ⌜also they said precisely after the same manner. 29. But there was one glory, and from it He did not change Himself. 30. And I saw when He ascended⌝ into the sixth heaven, ⌜and they worshipped and glorified Him⌝. 31. But in all the heavens the praise increased (in volume). 32. And I saw how He ascended into the seventh heaven, and all the righteous and all the angels praised Him. And then I saw Him sit down on the right hand of that Great Glory [1] whose glory I told you that I could not behold. 33. And also the angel of the Holy Spirit I saw sitting on the left hand.[2] 34. And this angel said unto me: " Isaiah, son of Amoz, *it is enough for thee*; ⌜for these are great things⌝; for thou hast seen what no child of flesh hath seen. 35. And thou wilt return into thy garment (of the flesh) until thy days are completed.[3] Then thou wilt come hither." 36. These things Isaiah saw and told unto all that stood before him, and they praised. And he spake to Hezekiah the King, ⌜and said⌝ : " I have spoken these things." 37. Both the end of this world; 38. And all this vision will be consummated in the last generations. 39. And Isaiah made him swear that he would not tell (it) to the people of Israel, nor give these words to any man to transcribe. 40. . . . *Such things* ye will read. And watch ye in the Holy Spirit in order that ye may receive your garments and thrones and crowns of glory which are laid up in the ⌜seventh⌝ heaven. 41. *On account of these visions and prophecies Sammael Satan sawed in sunder Isaiah the*

---

[1] Cf. ix. 37; x. 16.   [2] Cf. ix. 36.   [3] Cf. viii. 27.

son of Amoz, the prophet, by the hand of Manasseh. 42. And all these things Hezekiah delivered to Manasseh in the twenty-sixth year. 43. But Manasseh did not remember them nor place these things in his heart, but becoming the servant of Satan he was destroyed.

Here endeth the vision of Isaiah the prophet with his ascension.

TRANSLATIONS OF EARLY DOCUMENTS

A Series of texts important for the study of Christian origins, by various authors

UNDER THE JOINT EDITORSHIP OF
The Rev. W. O. E. OESTERLEY, D.D.
AND
The Rev. CANON G. H. BOX, M.A.

THE object of the Series is to provide short, cheap, and handy text-books for students, either working by themselves or in classes. The aim is to furnish in translations important texts unencumbered by commentary or elaborate notes, which can be had in larger works.

FIRST SERIES
Palestinian-Jewish and Cognate Texts (Pre-Rabbinic)

1. Aramaic Papyri. A. E. Cowley, Litt.D., Sub-Librarian of the Bodleian Library, Oxford.
2. The Wisdom of Ben-Sira (Ecclesiasticus). The Rev. W. O. E. Oesterley, D.D., Vicar of St. Alban's, Bedford Park, W.; Examining Chaplain to the Bishop of London.
3. The Book of Enoch. The Rev. R. H. Charles, D.D., Canon of Westminster.
4. The Book of Jubilees. The Rev. Canon Charles.
5. The Testaments of the Twelve Patriarchs. The Rev. Canon Charles.
6. The Odes and Psalms of Solomon. The Rev. G. H. Box, M.A., Rector of Sutton, Beds., Hon. Canon of St. Albans.
7. The Ascension of Isaiah. The Rev. Canon Charles.
8. The Apocalypse of Ezra (ii. Esdras). The Rev. Canon Box.
9. The Apocalypse of Baruch. The Rev. Canon Charles.
10. The Apocalypse of Abraham. The Rev. Canon Box.
11. The Testament of Abraham. The Rev. Canon Box.
12. The Assumption of Moses. The Rev. W. J. Ferrar, M.A., Vicar of Holy Trinity, East Finchley.

FIRST SERIES—*continued*

13. The Biblical Antiquities of Philo. M. R. James, Litt.D., F.B.A., Hon. Litt.D., Dublin, Hon. LL.D. St. Andrews, Provost of King's College, Cambridge.
14. Lost Apocrypha of the Old Testament. M. R. James, Litt.D.

Now Ready—Nos. 2, 3, 4, 5 and 8, 7 and 10 (in one vol.), 9 and 12 (in one vol.), and No. 13.

SECOND SERIES
Hellenistic-Jewish Texts

1. The Wisdom of Solomon. The Rev. Dr. Oesterley.
2. The Sibylline Oracles (Books iii–v). The Rev. H. N. Bate, M.A., Vicar of Christ Church, Lancaster Gate, W.; Examining Chaplain to the Bishop of London.
3. The Letter of Aristeas. H. St. John Thackeray, M.A., King's College, Cambridge.
4. Selections from Philo. J. H. A. Hart, M.A.
5. Selections from Josephus. H. St. J. Thackeray, M.A.
6. The Third and Fourth Books of Maccabees. The Rev. C. W. Emmet, B.D., Vicar of West Hendred, Oxon.
7. The Book of Joseph and Aseneth. Translated and edited from the Syriac text (for the first time in English) by E. W. Brooks.

Now Ready—Nos. 1 and 3.

THIRD SERIES
Palestinian-Jewish and Cognate Texts (Rabbinic)

*1. Pirqe Aboth. The Rev. Dr. Oesterley.
*2. Berakhoth. The Rev. A. Lukyn Williams, D.D.
*3. Yoma. The Rev. Canon Box.
*4. Shabbath. The Rev. Dr. Oesterley.
*5. Sanhedrin. Rev. H. Danby.
*6. Qimchi's Commentary on the Psalms (Book I, Selections). The Rev. R. G. Finch, B.D.

7. Tamid	10. Sopherim	13. Taanith
8. Aboda Zara	11. Megilla	14. Megillath Taanith
9. Middoth	12. Sukka	

* It is proposed to publish these texts first by way of experiment. If the Series should so far prove successful the others will follow.

Jewish Literature and Christian Origins:
  Vol. I. The Apocalyptic Literature.
    „   II. A Short Survey of the Literature of Rabbinical Judaism.
  By the Revs. Dr. Oesterley and Canon Box.

Jewish Uncanonical Writings: A popular Introduction. By the Rev. W. J. Ferrar.

SOCIETY FOR PROMOTING CHRISTIAN KNOWLEDGE
ENGLAND: 68 HAYMARKET, LONDON, S.W.
NEW YORK: THE MACMILLAN COMPANY

[1.1.18.